THE beauty DIARY
editorial edition

www.TheBeautyDiary.com

THE beauty DIARY
editorial edition

doable tips for the
BOSS LADY
who struggles to convert
basic beauty advice into everyday looks
&
AIN'T GOT
time to watch some over the top video!

BAILEY SESSOMS

Copyright©2016 by Bailey Orenia-Sessoms
Cover and Book Design by Bailey Sessoms
Cover Image by Okalinichenko

All rights reserved. This book, or parts thereof, may not be reproduced in any form without written permission from the author, except by a reviewer, who may quote brief passages in a review.

The Beauty Diary web site address is
http://www.TheBeautyDiary.com

First Edition

Bailey Sessoms, LLC paperback
ISBN: 978-0-9977130-7-7

Printed in the United States of America

Thank You God!

To the love of my life and my favorite person in the whole wide world.
Mommy loves you!

In memory of my grandma San Juan.
Thanks for introducing me to makeup.

the IDEA *factor*

When you tend to have a lot of ideas, it can be difficult to stay focused. I found my creative juices really begin to flow when I lie down and relax. They say that lying down decreases stress hormones, but I also know it's because GOD STARTS TO WORK WHEN YOU REST.

Let's get one thing clear:

I want you to know right off the bat that this book was not written to show my makeup skill as a professional makeup artist, but rather to educate you on what I do know and have learned as a makeup artist. In fact, none of the makeup was done by me. Yeah, you heard right and there is a very good reason why.

When I decided to write this book, I knew I wanted to do something different. When you normally read a beauty book written by a makeup artist or celebrity it's usually full of pictures of their life, their travels, and images of their celebrity friends and clients. I had no interest in recreating that wheel.

So I decided to deviate from the norm and offer up beauty advice in an editorial style, not as a chapter book. I decided to switch things up a bit and do it the same way magazines do where the writer (me) writes the story and the magazine pulls stock photography or hires a photographer and a style team to visually capture the story.

I opted for the more practical route of stock photography since I wasn't sittin' on a six-figure budget to produce this book. I wanted to offer up a collection of tips that are straight to the point, easy to follow, and practical to execute.

Now, don't expect tips on how to turn a plain Jane into an over the top diva {that ain't what I do}. And when we meet, don't expect me to walk around with a "beat" face to prove my makeup skills {ain't gonna happen}. However, you can expect some sassy, "Oh no, she didn't" truth along the way. So, if you're ultra-sensitive or a stick in the mud, you probably won't appreciate my real take on makeup.

With that said, I look forward to sharing with you, darling!

Here's A thought

"'Beauty' is not a word of truth; it is a word of judgement."

In a special video series segment for The Washington Post called "On Being," I was asked to share my experiences as a professional makeup artist and my perception of beauty. In this very candid segment, I spoke about my own personal struggles with society's preconceived notion of beauty and how I was teased about my physical appearance. All too often, women who have big breasts, curves, and voluptuous bottoms are slated for not being the conventional depiction of beauty. The beauty standards that were set in mainstream magazines and media troubled me greatly because when I looked in the mirror, I did not see a reflection of those same beauty standards.

Even in today's modern world, media still has a firm and unrelenting grip on our very notion of beauty. More often than not, they don't promote something as beautiful until it can be obtained by the masses, and yet very few embrace a culture's uniqueness, without making them a token. There comes a time when we must learn to let go of pre-established perceptions of beauty and own who we are — flaws and all.

As the adage goes, beauty is in the eyes of the beholder and, of course, depending on who's doing the looking, that definition will undoubtedly change. How many times have we stumbled upon an old photograph and reminisced about our past sense of style (or lack thereof) and thought to ourselves, "What the hell was I thinking!"? The reality is that we are no longer chasing that particular idea of beauty and, as such, we are able to see our (past) self in a much clearer light.

Let's face it, we all are insecure to some degree. For me, it was being called "bazooka lips," but when you lack self-love, you're more susceptible to accepting society's "beauty standards" and find yourself not liking who you are, year after year, because every year that standard changes.

So when the fads die down and women are no longer running to get lip injections and breast and butt implants, I will still have to stand in my truth and embrace my body and know that I, too, am beautiful.

To feel a need to conform to any standard of beauty means agreeing to judgement, but to compare ourselves to others, in any capacity, is an internal form of torture. You will never be "them" and equally, they will never be you.

Until you love yourself uniquely in the way that God has created you, you will never truly be happy. My intent in writing this is not to change who you are or give you tips on how to dramatically change your physical appearance, but rather it is meant to transform the way you see you. It is imperative to your inner happiness to have fun with ways that you can highlight your own sense of natural beauty.

Don't give others the power to decide who you are nor value you based on their beauty standards. Your self-worth should be determined by you and God.

Bailey

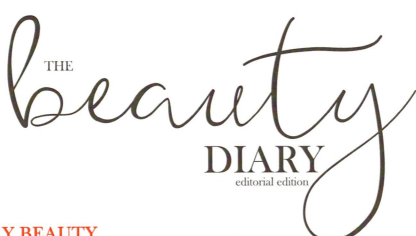

EVERYDAY BEAUTY

14 CODE BLUE! YOUR MAKEUP HAS EXPIRED

16 BEAUTY CHECK-IN

22 THE BRUSH OFF

23 CLEAN ME UP SCOTTIE

24 QUINTESSENTIAL TRAVEL KIT

26 FINE TUNE YOUR BEAUTY ROUTINE

28 SHOP LIKE A BEAUTY PRO

30 PRO APPROVED BEAUTY HACKS

32 MAKEUP THAT WORKS OVERTIME

33 8 BEAUTY CLASSICS OF MY OBSESSION

34 THE LIST: 7 NO-FAIL BEAUTY TIPS

35 AND THE EXPERTS SAY...

36 THE BEST BEAUTY YEAR OF YOUR LIFE

37 PHOTO FINISH: PICTURE PERFECT MAKEUP

38 PARTY PROOF YOUR LOOK

CONTENTS *continued...*

GIVING FACE

40 CORRECT & CONCEAL

42 IT'S ALL ABOUT THAT BASE

45 A FOUNDATION MISTAKE EVEN MAKEUP ARTISTS MAKE

46 THREE MOVES TO THE PERFECT FOUNDATION

47 THE TOP 5 FOUNDATION MISTAKES

48 THE ULTIMATE POWER OF POWDER

50 GLOWING RADIANT SKIN

52 CAMOUFLAGE THAT DOUBLE CHIN

53 PRINCIPLES OF CONTOURING

54 BLUSHING

56 CHEEKS THAT POP!

LIPS

60 LIP MATTERS

62 HELLO LIPS

64 THE PERFECT RED

66 A MATTE MADE IN HEAVEN

68 SOMETHING TO POUT ABOUT

69 OMBRÉ

LASHES

71 THE MISSING STEP TO THICKER LOOKING LASHES

72 FIVE STEPS TO BOMBSHELL LASHES

73 ROCKING LASHES WITH GLASSES

74 LASH WEAR & CARE

THE BEAUTY DIARY 12 EDITORIAL EDITION

CONTENTS *continued...*

76 THE POWER BROW

78 LINE LIKE A PRO

82 WINGING IT

84 WIDER BRIGHTER EYES

85 DODGE THESE EYESHADOW MISTAKES

86 PLAYING WITH COLOR

LOOKS

90 STATEMENT EYES

92 A NEW YORK MINUTE

94 SMOKIN'

96 COCKTAIL GLAM

98 VIBRANT THING

100 THE MINIMALIST

102 EBONY

CODE b!ue

Your Makeup Has Expired

Yeah I know, it's so not fair you have to throw out the lipstick that looks so darn good on you, but all good things must come to an end. Everything has an expiration date, including your makeup.

CODE BLUE! YOUR MAKEUP HAS EXPIRED

Crazy enough the FDA doesn't require cosmetic brands to print an expiration date on products. Some brands do print a POA (Period After Opening) symbol, which is a picture of a jar with a number and the letter M, which signifies how many months the product is good for after it's been open. Once a product is opened, it is exposed to different elements including bacteria and moisture, which will accelerate contamination.

POA
(Period After Opening) symbol

Even though there are general rules for the lifespan of a product, how long a product will be usable also depends on how it's made. The more preservatives a product contains, the longer the shelf life. Products that don't contain water will tend to last longer. Naturally, your organic and "all natural" products will expire much sooner, so you may want to monitor those products more often.

The POA date and these general guidelines listed are only ideal when your products have been used and kept under ideal conditions as directed on the packaging. But in the end, use common sense. If it looks bad or smells bad, toss it.

4-WEEKS
Makeup Sponge
I am not a fan of prolonged use. I prefer to keep my sponge for no more than a week, then I replace it. If this is not for you, I suggest using a foundation brush.

Razors
To increase usage, dry the blade after each use to minimize oxidation, which cases the blades to rust and become dull.

3 MONTHS
Mascara & Liquid Liners
Bacteria can live in makeup and can cause pink eye and even corneal infections.

6 - 12 MONTHS
Skincare
Skincare products that contain a SPF value or another type of "active" skincare ingredient are regulated by the FDA and contain expiration dates. But, products stating they have anti-aging or any other skin-changing benefits are not regulated. Store in a cool dry place.

Foundation & Concealer
You increase contamination when you repeatedly dip your brushes and fingers into liquid foundation. Evaluate the smell, consistency, and distribution of color. Consider tossing if the formulation has separated, is dried out, goes on unevenly, or leaves a streaky finish. Concealers can last up to 18-months.

12 – 24 MONTHS
Powders
Usually contain no water and last up to two years.

Lipstick & Lip Gloss
You know it's gone rancid when they start to change color, dry out, or develop a filmy application.

Eyeliner & Lip Liner
To ensure a clean tip, sharpen your liner after each use. If you ever develop an eye infection, be sure to discard all eye makeup to avoid reinfection.

Powder Eyeshadows
Are less prone to contamination because they do not contain water. Over time, shadows will lose their powdery consistency, making them more challenging to apply and blend.

Blush
Discard cream blushes after a year and powder blushes after two years.

Nail Polish
Store polishes away from sunlight and extreme temperatures, and ensure the top is secure. Before application, check for odors and discoloration as the formula thickens or hardens over time. Exposure to air and heat will accelerate this decline.

Perfume
Keep out of humidity and sunlight. Being exposed to these elements can alter the notes in a fragrance, which changes the overall scent.

NOW TRENDING
beauty check-in

You got the goods, just not the room. But it can be difficult to ditch colorful things that make your eyes open wide and your heart flutter. Here are five steps to help you sort through and eliminate your collection of expired products, makeup mishaps, duplicates, and trends of the past.

start here
Destination: ORGANIZED

Cleaning out your makeup stash ain't rocket science, but it can become complicated and time consuming if you don't have an itinerary to guide you along the way. Begin with knowing why you are taking this journey.

Have you found yourself saying any of the following?

I can't find my…

-

I didn't realize I already had this, now I have two.

-

Wow, I forgot I had this!

-

Don't know what I was thinking when I bought this.

Now that you know the "why," this goal should help you stay focused when organizing your products. Once you reach your destination, you will be able to find what you need and know what you have will look good on you.

get packin'

To get ready for your day of purge, you will need to make sure you have the necessary supplies on hand to ensure it goes off without a hitch. Here is a list of the items you will need.

- [ ] A clean work space big enough to accommodate all of your makeup and beauty supplies (and your friend's products too).

- [ ] Trash can to dispose of old, unusable products.

- [ ] A watch or the timer on your phone. (You'll see why you'll need this on the next page.)

- [ ] Four shoeboxes to sort products into keep, sell, donate, and recycle. Grab them from your closet as they are only being used temporarily. Feel free to line the boxes with a bag to avoid getting makeup on your shoes when finished.

- [ ] A pen and sticky notes to label each box.

- [ ] A mirror. Use a hand mirror if you are not doing your purge in a room with a mirror. This will save time from having to run back and forth when trying to see if a color works.

- [ ] And don't forget the bottle of wine and tasty treats.

book your reservation + invite a friend

Without question, the best time to book your reservation for a beauty purge is on the weekend. What will make this quest even better is to invite a friend whose opinion you trust to keep the process movin'. This is a great time to get your friend's input on what works and doesn't work.

But who really wants to spend their day off helping a friend clean? To give your friend a little motivation, invite her over for a beauty check-in and have her bring her makeup stash along too. Let her know that you will be serving cocktails and tasty treats. You can even end the day by giving each other mini makeovers.

THE BEAUTY DIARY 17 EDITORIAL EDITION

check-in + unpack

Today is the big day and it's time to check in and unpack. Keep in mind this is not an extended stay.

You are checking in for a cleanse where you have to put it all on the table, literally. Don't try to organize what you have before you decide what to keep. You will only be successful if you clear out the unwanted and unusable items first. Grab everything out of your makeup bag, bathroom vanity, linen closet, and even your purse, and arrange it in the following categories.

Eyes
Lips
Face
Tools

After sorting into the above categories, separate the products in each category based on how often you wear them.

Always
Sometimes
Never

yea or nah

After your power purge you can add the products you selected into your keep box. Next, look to see if any of your products have expired. Does it have an unpleasant order or discoloration? If yes, separate what should be trashed and what can be recycled.

Now it's time to sort through each item and ask yourself the following questions:

Have I worn it in the last 3-months?
-
Is it currently in style and does it reflect my current sense of style?
-
If I were shopping at the counter right now, would I buy it?
-
Do I feel confident when I wear it?

If the answer is no, it's gotta go.
As you go through each product you can begin to add them to your keep, sell, donate, recycle, and trash boxes. (*Only sell a product that has never been open.*)

power-purge

Now it's time to power purge. Set your timer because you only have 10 seconds to grab the items you absolutely love. Ready? Set. Go!

here's the flow

Collect all your products into one pile and sort them into the following categories.

How often do you wear them? {Always, Sometimes, Never}
Add the products you always wear to your keep box, but make sure none of these items have expired and your friend agrees that these products works for you. Add any duplicate items to the sell or donate box.

With the remaining items, answer the "Yea or Nah" questions on the previous page. If you answer no to any of these other questions, it is time to purge. Place products that can be turned in for product credit into the recycle box. You may sell or donate any unopened products, but be sure they have not expired. Place all other items in the trash.

The Layover

There are going to be a few items you are not sure if you should keep. When in doubt, I suggest holding on to them for no more then 30 days, but make a firm date when you will purge them if you don't use them. During this 30 day layover, I suggest wearing each item a few times to see if you get any compliments. If the reviews aren't great or if you never use them within the allotted time, then it's time to purge.

Unpack

Now that you have successfully purged, it is time to assess your beauty storage space and unpack your keep box. The key to this process is to organize your products so they are easily assessable. Be realistic about the space you actually have in order to avoid creating clutter.

Think about items you use every day, once a week, or only on special occasions, and what items you carry in your purse.

Store every day and weekly items within arms' reach, like in a vanity drawer or medicine cabinet. For special occasions or seasonal colors, store them in a container under the sink or in the linen closet.

If you tend to take your daily makeup with you, store it in a mini makeup bag that fits into your purse. This will avoid mishaps from makeup getting all over your things.

make it easy...

Store items in a location you frequent. Remember, out of sight, out of mind.

-

Keep makeup in a clear container to find what you need faster.

-

To easily identify items, store like items together. Keep eyeliners and lip liners separate, likewise with eyeshadow and blush.

-

Sort items by color too. This is a great idea if you have numerous shades of lipstick. It makes it a lot easier when looking for a particular shade.

-

Keeping products off counter tops makes for a clutter free space. But, if you insist on storing items on top of your vanity, treat your makeup like a cosmetic counter you would see in a high-end department store. Purchase a makeup organization storage container to help keep things organized.

-

Only buy storage items after you have decided what you are going to keep and have determined how much storage space you have.

Lasting Memories

After a beauty purge, you want the results to last. These tips will keep you on track for years to come.

stop splurging

Beauty blogs and magazines are constantly comparing products you can splurge on versus alternative products that will save you money. Purchasing these items only makes sense if you are currently looking to replenish a product or if you are in need of a new look.

swap it out

When you know your storage space is limited, you should keep this in mind when purchasing new products. To keep your beauty stash in check, agree for every new item you buy you have to swap it out with a current item. This will make you think hard about whether the new product is worth it.

limit spending

You can't move in two directions at the same time, so keep in mind you didn't purge only to go shopping. This is where I challenge you to guesstimate how much you spent on the items in all of your boxes. How much money are you spending (or wasting) on products? The amount might surprise you.

Define Your Style

We usually don't give much thought to defining our beauty style. Think about what colors look best on you, and how much time your daily lifestyle allows you to invest in your beauty routine. Flip through magazines and blogs for inspiration on classic looks that coordinate with the image you want to project. You may also want to consult with a professional makeup artist to help guide you and to offer professional insight.

where to castoff

DONATE
You can donate unopened beauty products to women and children in need. Be sure to visit each organization's site to view details on the products they accept. Also contact your local shelter.
(BeautyBus.org, StJude.org, DressForSuccess.org, SuccessInStyle.org)

GIVE or SWAP
I am a firm believer charity starts at home, so think about any family members or close friends who may need your unopened products. You can even ask them to gather all their unused products and invite them over for a swap party.

REUSE or RECYCLE
Recycling your beauty products can be twofold. Provided they have not expired, you can always mix colors together to make a new color. Some companies accept empty packaging for recycling purposes and some also offer a free product in return. Visit each site for details, using the keyword "recycle."
(MacCosmetics.com, Origins.com, Aveda.com)

SELL
Selling or buying unused makeup can be tricky because of the possible contamination hazards. Many makeup products don't have an expiration date printed on them so it is safer to purchase items from someone you know, as they are more likely to be honest about when they purchased the product.

Sure, as a makeup artist I have a slew of makeup brushes, but the truth is I don't even use them all. With that being said, there is no reason to feel you have to have a plethora of makeup brushes to create basic looks. Since the life of an artist sometimes requires me to improvise, I've learned that the key is selecting brushes that can be used for different product applications. Here are my top makeup brushes and when and where I like to use them.

the 'BRUSH off

contour
Angled brush allows for a defined application.
USE: Contour, blush, and bronzer highlight.

foundation
A synthetic hair brush that yields a smooth foundation application.
USE: May be used to apply concealer and foundation, and to blend cream products.

spoolie
Has a tapered head and soft bristles for grooming brows and separating lashes.
USE: Evens out filled in brow color. Removes clumps after applying mascara.

fluff
Applies color quickly and easily to the eyes, blends away harsh lines, great for the crease.
USE: Eye shadow, applying loose powder around eyes, lips, and nose area.

shadow
Basic eyeshadow brush used to apply color to eyelids and brow bone.
USE: Eyelids and brow bone.

smudge
Creates sharp lines but its shape also allows you blend away harsh lines if desired.
USE: Great for both gel eyeliner and powder eyeshadow as a liner, and brow brush.

lip
The firm synthetic hairs allow for a precision application for outlining and applying lip color.
USE: Applying and blending lip color, cake eye liner, and concealer.

CLEAN
me up scottie, in...
HOW TO CLEAN YOUR TOOLS

3 Wet each brush and place a drop of gentle shampoo (I like using a baby shampoo) in the palm of your hands.

2 Rub the brush around in a circular motion to release the embedded makeup. Repeat as needed until the water runs clear of makeup, then rinse.

1 Press out excess water with a towel and reshape brushes by brushing them across the towel. Lay flat with the brush hairs resting over the edge of the counter or table.

DIRTY BRUSHES CAN LEAVE YOU WITH:

- Clogged pores due to dirt and bacteria.

- A poor makeup application because of product buildup.

- Premature wrinkles resulting from exposing skin to oxidative stress, which compromises antioxidant defenses due to free radicals.

- A dusty environment filled with dead skin cells, dirt, oil, and bacteria.

NEVER

- Soak your brushes. This will loosen the glue that keeps the hairs attached to the brush.

- Share your makeup brushes. You can catch a viral infection like conjunctivitis (better known as pinkeye) and even a staph infection.

- Go more than a week without cleaning your brushes if you use them every day.

ALWAYS

- Clean your other makeup tools too. After each use, wipe down your eyelash curler and lash guards with a makeup wipe to remove caked on mascara, and then clean them and your tweezers with rubbing alcohol to remove bacteria.

QUICK BEAUTY TIP

Need to use the same makeup brush to apply a different color and want to instantly remove eyeshadow from your makeup brushes? Swipe it across a **stippling sponge**. (This technique should not be used as a substitute for cleaning your brushes.)

QUINTESSENTIAL
TRAVEL KIT

Consider these twelve items as the bare necessities to assembling the ultimate packing list for your on-the-go beauty stash.

QUINTESSENTIAL
TRAVEL KIT

Consider this list the ultimate makeup kit for beginners too!

— face —

- **PRIMER**
  Helps your foundation application go on smoother. But be sure to select a primer formulated to work with your foundation. *(See page 45)*

- **CONCEALER**
  Choose a formula creamy enough to cover under eye circles and blemishes.

- **FOUNDATION**
  No matter how many flaws you may have, a light application will do. Too much foundation will leave a cakey and unnatural looking finish. If you only need a light coverage, try a tinted moisturizer instead. *(See page 43)*

- **TRANSLUCENT POWDER**
  Apply a light dusting of powder to set makeup and control shine.

- **BRONZER OR BLUSH**
  Select a warm tone and brush it lightly up along the cheekbone to add a pop of color to your cheeks.

— tools —

- **TWEEZERS**
  Clean up stray facial and brow hairs. Also the perfect tool to apply your false lashes.

- **MINI BRUSH SET**
  To keep things simple, purchase a travel brush set that includes blush/powder, shadow, crease, lip, and eyeliner brushes.

- **FOUNDATION SPONGE**
  Minimize facial irritation by using a disposable, latex free sponge. Discard after use to avoid the potential risk of adding bacteria onto the skin along with residue from previous makeup applications.

— eyes & lips —

- **EYELINER PENCIL**
  Use a classic black or brown liner pencil or opt for your darker shade eyeshadow as a liner and line along the lashes to define and enhance your eyes.

- **BROW PENCIL/POWDER**
  Apply with a light hand and opt for a powder or pencil with a powdery finish to avoid a shiny, unnatural finish.

- **EYESHADOW & LIP PALETTE**
  A palette is a great option if you're not sure what colors to select. They offer a collection of shades that complement each other, which helps eliminate the guesswork.

- **MASCARA**
  Define your eyes by enhancing your lashes with mascara. Wipe off excess mascara to prevent clumps. Select black, but if your lashes are blonde go with dark brown.

shopping list...

- _____
- _____
- _____
- _____

THE BEAUTY DIARY — EDITORIAL EDITION

fine tune
your beauty routine

fine tune
your beauty routine

"Some would say there is a proper order to applying your beauty products. I say it's all relative."

When it comes to a skincare and makeup routine, these are the steps I use. However, if you have a routine that's working for you, or your dermatologist has directed you otherwise, then stick with your current routine.

MAKEUP

When applying your makeup remember to apply all cream base products first before applying powder.

Face Primer

•

Eyeshadow Primer

•

Corrective Concealer

•

Foundation
(If your foundation has a sunscreen, then this amount will be the total level of protection.)

•

Concealer
(Some may prefer to apply their concealer first.)

•

Powder

•

Brows

•

Eyeshadow

•

Eyeliner

•

Mascara

•

False Lashes

•

Contouring Powder/Bronzer

•

Powder Blush

•

Highlighter

•

Lip Liner

•

Gloss

•

Finishing/Fixing Mist

SKINCARE

Cleanser
(Use a water-soluble cleanser appropriate for your skin type.)

•

Scrub
(Avoid using abrasive scrubs with topical prescription medications, which make micro-tears on the skin's surface.)

•

Mask

•

Toner

•

Acne Spot Treatment

•

Anti-aging

•

Eye Cream

•

Moisturizer

•

Sunscreen
(Opt for a broad-spectrum sunscreen rated SPF 25 or greater.)

SHOP PRO
like a beauty

– 1 –
Buy Sets And Palettes
Not only will you save lots on money, but brands also offer special collection palettes to help eliminate the guesswork around coordinating colors.

– 2 –
Do Your Homework
Instead of splurging on high-end brands, search the web for product dupes from brands that offer the exact or very similar colors for half the price. Also, while in the store, use your phone to quickly look up product reviews.

– 3 –
Go On A Sample Spree
If you are looking to build your makeup collection but want to minimize makeup mishaps, visit the makeup counter and ask for samples of foundations, loose powders and shadows, lipstick, and perfumes before you buy.

– 4 –
Buy Discounted Gift Cards
Some people sell their gift cards at discounted prices for cash. Be sure to check the balance with the store and make sure the security shield on the back of the card isn't scratched off.

– 5 –
Ask A Friend
Bring along a friend whose opinion you trust. Their input will ensure you're choosing a great looking product for a realistic price. And don't be shy, pick up the phone and ask your friends if they have any unopened makeup they don't want.

SHOP *like a beauty* PRO

GOLDEN RULES
to Remember Before You Buy

Always apply your makeup in natural light, so before you buy, take a hand mirror and go to a window to reveal its true colors. Test your foundation shade twice a year because your skin tone changes over time. You will need a darker shade for warmer months and a lighter shade for colder months. If it ain't broke, then don't try to fix it, especially if the product continues to bring you compliments. It's great to discover a product that you can consider a classic and can be your go-to item when pressed for time. A brand's resident makeup artists are usually knowledgeable and well trained. Ask what formulations work best on your skin and what colors to consider. Develop a good rapport and they'll spill the beans on upcoming promotions and even offer up a few extra samples. When in doubt, say no to the any product that doesn't call your name and make you feel all giddy inside. It's always best to buy that one product that looks damn good even if you have to splurge, rather then a few that don't do you justice. Double check to make sure you aren't about to buy a shade very similar to the one you already have. We like to stick with what we know, but there's no point in wasting money in the process.

> "Splurging on a new look every year or so is totally realistic. It keeps you and your sense of style feeling fresh and helps avoid falling into a beauty rut."

– 6 –
Avoid Paying Full Price

All your favorite beauty stores have a clearance section or aisle that gets restocked weekly, and usually includes beauty tools, cosmetics, and beauty products. When shopping online, always visit the sale page first.

– 7 –
Travel Size It

If you are on a budget, invest in travel size brushes. They're half the size and half the price. But avoid travel size products as they tend to cost more per ounce.

– 8 –
Seasonal Sales

Many cosmetic brands and store have seasonal sales to promote the transition of seasons. The usual offers are a discount or free gift with purchase.

– 9 –
Free Samples

Some brands offer free samples when you make a purchase over a certain dollar amount. This also rings true when you sign up for their loyalty club where you can accumulate points toward free products.

– 10 –
Return Policies

Since return policies vary by store, be sure to know how and what can be returned before making a purchase. Some allow you to return products with no questions asked, while others implement a strict no refund or exchange policy on opened items.

PRO

APPROVED BEAUTY HACKS

CUSTOM
NAIL POLISH

Crush eyeshadow into a fine powder (or use loose eye shadow) and funnel into a bottle of clear nail polish. Shake until color is distributed evenly in the bottle. Voilà!

LIP STAIN OR
LINER

Don't let the eyeshadow you just dropped go to waste. If it makes a perfect lip color, add the crushed shadow to a small container and mix with a little petroleum jelly. If your eyeshadow looks best on the eyes, then use it as an eyeliner by using a wet liner brush to apply.

MAGIC WAND

When your mascara expires, recycle the wand. Clean and use as a brow brush to fill in brows, or spray with hair spray to keep brows in place. You can also recycle the wand from your favorite high-end brand and use it with your favorite drugstore brand.

BLOTTING
TISSUE

The next time you're at the dollar store, grab a pack of coffee filters and turn them into the perfect super absorbent blotting tissue. Cut into sheets or other unique shapes and bring along to pat down the shine.

THE BEAUTY DIARY 30 EDITORIAL EDITION

WATERPROOF EYELINER

Turn your waterproof mascara into waterproof eyeliner. Take an eyeliner brush (a lip brush works too) and swipe across your mascara wand. Wipe off any excess mascara before lining your eyes.

the BROWNS have it

The color brown truly gives you options. Depending on your skin tone and hair color, grab a taupe or rich brown matte eyeshadow (or pencil) and use it to fill in your brows and to line your eyes. A darker shade of brown is also great for creating a smoky look or applying to the crease of the eye for definition.

RAZOR SMOOTH
Before you throw out your razor, use it to remove fabric pills, better known as fuzz. Lay clothes on a flat hard surface and gently shave across your garment.

SCENTED BODY LOTION

THE BRUSH OFF

If you ever wanted a body lotion that smelled like your favorite perfume, or if you are down to the last few drops and want to make it last, then grab some unscented body lotion, scoop some into an empty container, and spray with your favorite scent. Mix well before using and only make enough for a day's use to minimize product waste.

If you're looking for a soft nail brush to clean under your nails, just recycle your old soft bristle toothbrush. If you feel the need to kill those bad breath cooties first, simply soak in a cup of boiling hot water.

Bold Shadow & Liner
Eyeshadow + Water
To create the perfect defining eyeliner (and to avoid product contamination), I like to lightly scrape off a little shadow and wet my flat makeup brush. To create a bold eyeshadow I use a soft wet shadow brush. Either way, be sure to wipe off excess shadow before you apply.

Eye Shadow
Eyeliner + Brush
For a chic night out, pull out your favorite eyeliner and give your eyes some intense definition. Fill in your lids, smudge in using your fingertip, and blend with a soft shadow brush. Set with translucent powder.

MAKEUP THAT WORKS OVERTIME
STREAMLINE YOUR BEAUTY ROUTINE WITH PRODUCTS THAT PULL DOUBLE DUTY

Sheer Lip Color
Lip Gloss + Lipstick
To create a sheer lip color, first apply a clear lip gloss, then apply lipstick.

Liquid Foundation
Cream Foundation + Primer
Mix one part cream or stick foundation with one part primer. This will turn your foundation into a liquid consistency. For a thinner consistency, add a little more primer.

Lips That Pop
Shimmery Shadow + Lipstick
Want lips that pop? In a small container, mix a little bit of shimmery shadow like rosy peach, pink champagne, or rosy lilac with your existing lip color.

8 beauty CLASSICS of my obsession

Over the years I have developed an intimate relationship with these classic beauties. One thing I know for sure, if a product doesn't hold up to its end of the bargain it won't be around for long.

1 TWEEZERMAN
I've owned my pair of Tweezerman Tweezers for over three years and they get used daily. Between arching my brows and plucking stubborn facial hairs, I still haven't sent them in for sharpening.

2 CHESTNUT LIP LINER
This is one liner from MAC that looks great on any skin tone, especially if you have yellow undertones. When a lip color isn't quite right, the brown adds warmth, creating the perfect color balance.

3 ST. IVES
I get all giddy just thinking about their apricot scrub. I've been using this stuff since I was a teenager. Nothing is better than having smooth skin before you apply your makeup.

4 VASELINE
Petroleum jelly has become a staple in many of our medicine cabinets, but sometimes we forget that it is a topical ointment with healing properties. I use this along with Eucerin's Aquaphor to help keep my eczema at bay.

5 NOXZEMA
Before makeup wipes there was cold cream. I don't know what the directions say, but for a deep cleaning I like to wash my face then apply Noxzema, wait until it dries (almost like a facial mask), then rinse.

6 CARMEX
This tube of lube is awesome. When I first started using it, it made my lips tingle with a warming sensation. Now that I'm addicted the sensation is pretty much gone but it still leaves my lips soft and supple. Apply first, then do your makeup. Your lips will be softer by the time you are ready to apply your lipstick.

7 MAYBELLINE
Great Lash Clear Mascara has a true cult following and I'm first in line. I have a love affair with this transparent tube because I can use it to keep my brows in place and to make my lashes look nice and wet like I just stepped out of the shower.

8 A BERKELEY CALIFORNIA SPA
There are some beauty experiences you never forget. For me it was a couple's massage at the Claremont Club & Spa many years ago. My friend at the time said I was snoring. As I looked at my massage therapist in doubt, she kindly confirmed. This was the first and only time a massage felt so good.

THE BEAUTY DIARY 33 EDITORIAL EDITION

the list

7 NO FAIL BEAUTY TIPS

1. Make It Pop
Don't want to wear makeup, but still want to make a statement at a holiday party or special event? Select a bold lip color like red or pink to add some pop to your style.

2. Go Dark
Scrap the white lash glue that comes with your eyelash set. It doesn't dry completely clear and reflects light. Opt for a black lash glue, which gives the appearance of black eyeliner when dry.

3. SPF Doesn't Add Up
Wearing various layers of sunscreen products will not increase the total level of protection. The last Sun Protection Factor (SPF) level you apply determines your total sun protection. For example, if you apply a moisturizer with SPF 15 and then a sunscreen with SPF 30, the total protection is SPF 30, not SPF 45.

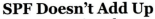

4. Shimmering Highlights
To highlight and define your brows in a hurry, apply shimmery eyeshadow in cream or soft pink on your brow bone. This will make your brows look more defined, and add a pop of color too.

5. Master The Tap
When it comes to powder based products like eyeshadow, loose powder, brow powder, and blush, it's important to tap off excess product onto a tissue or paper towel. This eliminates over-application and allows you to build color intensity gradually.

7. Treat Your Feet
Petroleum jelly has healing properties and works wonders on dry feet. Right before bed, apply a moisturizer, rub on some petroleum jelly, and then slip on a comfy pair of cotton socks. This works well right after a pedicure. I tend to do this several times a week, especially when it's cold outside.

6. Less Is More
Remember when you were younger, and you wore makeup to look older? Then note, wearing too much makeup does just that: it makes you look older.

and the Experts say...

Since eyelid skin is the thinnest skin in the body and shows age most quickly, use an eye cream morning and night. Choose an eye cream with high levels of peptides and antioxidants. Peptides stimulate collagen production, which helps to minimize fine lines. While antioxidants bind to free radicals and inactivate them so they benefit your skin.
-**DR. DEBRA JALIMAN,**
Dermatologist/Author of "Skin Rules: Trade Secrets From a Top New York Dermatologist"
@debrajalimanmd
(Featured in Allure, InStyle, Vogue, Elle, Glamour)

Don't solely depend on your stylist to educate you, do some research on your own hair texture and on which products will strengthen and grow your hair.
-**CHARLENE BROWN,**
Celebrity Hairstylist
@CharleneBrown
(Clients include Leonardo DiCaprio, Tia Mowry, Wendy Raquel Robinson, Omarosa Manigault)

Moisturize twice a day and use sunscreen! Pay attention to your skin and adjust your moisturizer accordingly during seasonal shifts. Your skin will thank you for it with less wrinkles, sagging, and other signs of aging.
-**ALANA RIVERA,**
Etta + Billie
@EttaAndBillie
(Featured in InStyle, Japan Vogue, WWD, Refinery 29, Parents)

When it comes to fragrance, wear what speaks to your soul! Having a signature scent is nice, but a perfume is a potion that transcends time and space! So cultivate a stellar collection that speaks to you.
-**MINDY YANG,**
Sensory Expert & Curator of TheArtOfLiving.Earth
@GoDolceVita
(Featured in Vanity Fair, Vogue, Elle, Allure, WWD)

the best beauty year of your life

JANUARY
REASSESS YOUR ROUTINE
Reflect on what beauty routines worked and which ones need a little tweaking. Take time to assess what new purchases you may need to make for the warmer months ahead, and remember to replace your mascara by setting a reminder on your phone to replace it every three months.

FEBRUARY
PICK THE PERFECT RED
Every woman should own a classic red lipstick. The color red can transitions with the occasion. You can rock it with a power suit, play it up for a night on the town, and spice it up for a romantic evening. Go for a red based gloss for color that's less intense.

MARCH
POWER NAP
Skip the caffeine. A power nap will help boost your memory, creativity, and energy level. For most people, a 20 minute midday power nap is optimal. Do not go over 30 minutes or you might enter deep sleep and then feel groggy, and generally worse off.

APRIL
FIND YOUR BALANCE
With the season of new beginnings, relax, relate, and release the stress away with a massage. Studies have shown that a massage can help sooth anxiety and depression; reduce muscle pain, swelling, fatigue, nausea, and the number of migraines; and it also improves sleep.

MAY
BLOCK THE SUN
Replace your bottle of sunscreen, which loses its effectiveness within a year. Don't forget that UVR rays are just as strong in the winter. Unprotected exposure can increase premature skin aging and suppression of the immune system. And when you damage the genetic material in your skin cells, you're at risk for skin cancer.

JUNE
CLARIFY YOUR LOCKS
A clarifying shampoo can repair the damage caused by the summer's elements by stripping away dirt, oils, chlorine, salt water, and styling-product buildup on your scalp and shaft. Unclogging hair follicles and cuticles allows moisture and nutrients to penetrate into the hair. Repeat monthly.

JULY
RECONSIDER YOUR FOUNDATION
With warmer months comes darker skin, so use a darker shade for hotter months and a lighter shade for colder months. Your skin tone may also change over time, so be sure to test your foundation shade twice a year. Reassess your concealer too.

AUGUST
MAKE SCENTS
August tends to be the hottest month of the summer, and sometimes wearing makeup, can be less than ideal. If you ever opt not to wear makeup stop by the cosmetic counter to try a new floral scent for an added girlie touch.

SEPTEMBER
GOOD TIMES
Being beautiful is also about being happy. Life becomes boring when you stay in the confines of what you already know. Try something new each month, like throwing soap in a fountain, carving your name in a tree, taking a long drive and seeing where you end up, leaving a positive note on someone's car, or playing hide and seek in Ikea.

OCTOBER
CHECK THE BOOBS
Breast Cancer awareness month acts as a great reminder to have your annual mammogram (or during your birthday month). After your visit, remember to perform your monthly self-examinations for early detection. Also, if you've had skin cancer, have new spots on the skin, or notice any moles that change size, shape, or color, take this time to consult with your dermatologist.

NOVEMBER
MANI-PEDI STOCK UP
Things start to slow down during the colder months and this is the time of the year when salons and spas tend to offer major discounts on mani-pedi services, with gift certificates and package deals.

DECEMBER
RENEW YOUR SKIN
Exfoliating helps unclog pores and removes dead skin cells, which is beneficial for skin renewal. Exfoliate no more than three times a week. If your skin becomes irritated, inflamed, or you develop acne breakouts, this is a clear indication of over exfoliating. To minimize dryness, take quick warm showers and apply a rich moisturizer.

PHOTO *finish:*
Picture Perfect Makeup

When applying makeup for the camera, there are some makeup rules you need to reconsider. Knowing camera-ready makeup isn't about heavy makeup or over the top colors, it's more about knowing what the camera (and the flashes) are going to reveal. I gathered together some tips to help get your next shots picture perfect.

Be sure to clean, exfoliate, and moisturize with an oil-free moisturizer to ensure the best canvas for your makeup application. Don't try anything new in skincare or haircare products right before a shoot to avoid breakouts and potential style mishaps.

~

Use a T-Zone Mattifier to eliminate shine on your forehead, nose, cheeks, and any other areas that tend to shine. Also, be sure to apply primer to your eyelids to keep the color from creasing.

~

Avoid SPF foundation, which tends to reflect a whitish hue on camera.

~

Applying makeup in the light you will be seen in is always a golden rule especially when it comes to taking pictures. Before you're almost ready to take your pictures, snap a selfie in the photographer's light to make sure you like what you see. Make adjustments if necessary.

~

Natural and nude lip colors can look washed out in photos, so select a shade that has more rose, pink, or plum hues.

~

Fill brows with brow powder or pomade versus a pencil, (Unless you've got your technique down and know how to make flawless hair strokes with a pencil.) A brow powder allows for more imperfection then a pencil.

~

Use matte shadows, and avoid shimmery products with pearlescent or white tones, which reflect light and can make you look washed out and at times ashy. They do not convert well in photos. You can use then sparingly to highlight some areas like the brow bone.

~

Line and define. Be sure to make your features pop by lining your eyes. Like they say, smile with your eyes. The eyes are the window to the soul.

~

Powder neck (and check if it is exposed) so the flash reflects light evenly.

~

Less is not more. Pictures don't reflect what you look like in real life. What appears overdone in person will pop on camera.

pARty
proof your look

There's nothing quite like sweat to ruin a great party or just a day out. With the heat on full blast, the very thought of putting on foundation can make you cringe. I say this is the perfect time to give your skin a break. But if you insist on wearing makeup, use these tips to keep it cute and avoid looking like a hot, runny mess.

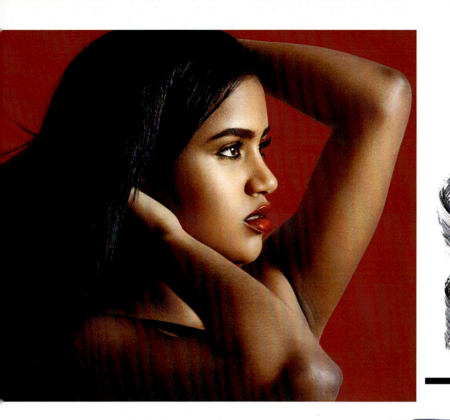

pARty
proof your look

EYES

Use waterproof mascara and eyeliner.

Dab a pea size amount of eyeshadow primer to keep eyeshadow from creasing.

FACE & CHEEKS

As I mentioned earlier in the book, be sure to blot away excess oils after applying moisturizer and again after applying foundation.

~

Spritz your face with makeup fixing spray before applying makeup, to extend makeup wear and keeps it from melting and settling into fine lines. Spray after makeup to set makeup.

~

Apply face primer to keep your face from getting shiny throughout the day. Its invisible layer helps to create a smooth canvas for your makeup application and keeps it looking fresher longer.

~

Use an oil-free foundation for obvious reasons.

~

Use a sheer amount of concealer to prevent it from creasing when you sweat.

~

Use a cream or gel blush, which requires a little more blending but is highly pigmented.

~

Press (don't wipe) loose powder over face to set foundation.

LIPS

Apply a **lip primer** to give color staying power and a more vivid color. Try using a **creamy lip stain** that is smudge proof and water resistant for easy application and touchups.

BROWS

For staying power, use a **waterproof eyeliner pencil** for filling in brows. If you have better luck filling in brows with a brush, use a **waterproof brow pomade** instead.

~

Set with powder. I like setting brows with a **light dusting of loose powder**, not only to remove the shine that may be left behind from filling them in, but also to help them look more realistic.

~

To keep brows in place, I grab my **clear mascara**. Be sure to wipe off the excess mascara with a tissue first.

THE BEAUTY DIARY EDITORIAL EDITION

CORRECT & CONCEAL

SHADES ON THE COLOR WHEEL THAT MAKE SKIN LOOK FLAWLESS

Whatever problem you may be facing, dark spots and patches, under eye circles, reddish patches and pimples, or washed out looking skin, there are some basic application techniques you need to remember.

EXPERT TIPS:

Make sure skin is well hydrated

—

Only apply to the affected area

—

Apply a very small amount in sheer layers

—

Never apply in a circular motion (the buffing technique) as this will move product away from the targeted area and may further irritate the skin.

—

If you need to correct a large area of the skin, apply the corrector first, then your foundation or concealer.

—

To cover smaller areas like dark spots and red pimples, apply your foundation first then apply corrector in sheer layers with a brush in a tapping motion (do not wipe on as this will move the product to other areas), only to the areas that need it. Then apply a little foundation (in the same formula as the corrector) that matches your skin tone.

—

Wait a few minutes to allow corrector to dry.

—

Finish with loose powder.

DARK SPOTS & PATCHES

Peach (fair skin)
Apricot (medium skin)
Orange (deep skin)

DARK CIRCLES

Peach (fair skin)
Orange (tan to dark skin)
Red (deep skin)

Apply a hydrating eye cream. Use a creamy texture corrector to accommodate the thin, sensitive skin around the eyes. Next apply your concealer in the same shade as your skin tone or one shade lighter. Then finish with loose powder using a small fluff brush.

REDNESS
reddish patches and pimples

Green (intense redness)
Yellow (mild redness)

DULLNESS

Pink (fair skin)
Purple (medium skin),
Orange/Apricot (deep skin)

If you skin looks yellow or grey, you may want to consider using a brightening corrector product.

Art was my favorite class in school and thank God I was paying attention when we learned about color theory. Who knew the key to neutralizing imperfections would lie on the opposite side of the color wheel? And when applied in small amounts, these shades provide a flawless canvas that transforms your complexion, so there's no need for a heavy concealer or foundation. Bye-bye, cake face!

WHEN TO USE
I believe you should elect to use a concealer only when your foundation does not provide adequate coverage. One of the biggest mistakes it grabbing for a concealer to cover under eye circles when your foundation will do.

THE FORMULA
I prefer using a creamy concealer like a stick foundation as it provides a fuller coverage. Liquid concealers tend to travel and fade quickly. Stay away from concealers that are oily, thick, or dry.

RIGHT SHADE
Opt for a yellow or golden based concealer, not white. Typically, it should be the same shade, no more than one shade lighter than your foundation. Anything lighter will be too light.

APPLYING
Warm the product on the back of your hand and apply with your fingers using a tapping motion (or a small-tipped concealer brush) up to the lower lash line and the inner corner of your eyes. Set concealer with powder using a circular sponge.

REMEMBER...
A little goes a long way!

CONCEALER
IF YOU HAVE RELATIVELY EVEN SKIN YOU MAY NOT NEED A COLOR CORRECTING CONCEALER. SOMETIMES A CREAMY FOUNDATION OR CONCEALER WILL DO THE

IT'S ALL ABOUT THAT BASE

FOUNDATION TYPES:

Liquid Foundation
provides a light to medium coverage and comes in oil-free and moisturizing.

Cream Foundation
is usually found in a compact or a stick and yields a heavier coverage.

Cream-to-Powder
can provide a sheer-to-full, buildable coverage.

Mousse Foundation
offers a medium to heavy coverage.

Iridescent Foundation
gives an added glow to your complexion.

SHAKE FIRST
When using liquid foundation, shake the bottle well before applying to ensure ther heavier particles of the foundation are blended well. If there is a noticeable amount of separation, it is time for it to be replaced.

TRY, TRY AGAIN
Try to buy foundation at a department store or book an appointment with a professional makeup artist so you can get expert advice for choosing the best formula and shade. Keep in mind that it may take you a couple of tries before you get it right.

GIVE IT TIME
Give a product time to set (dry) before you apply another product.

DRY, YET HOT
If you have dry skin in warmer months, opt for a heavier moisturizer with an oil-free foundation to avoid a heavy, weighted down feel.

FOUNDATION HAS COME A LONG WAY

When it comes to foundation, I think just about everyone has a horror story to share. Mine was eons ago when I was walking to the bus stop on my way home from junior high and I noticed this woman whose appearance seemed quite off, but I couldn't quite put my finger on it. As I got closer I realized she was wearing too much makeup and to make matters worse her foundation was way too light. I found myself just staring (along with a few other folks), wondering how in the world she could have thought that was okay. I mean, you would have thought she was getting ready for a theatrical appearance as a Geisha. I will give her the benefit of the doubt because finding the perfect shade foundation for women of color has been a continuous struggle. Here you will see the key is to also know the right process for selecting the perfect shade and formula to fit your skin's color, undertone, and skin type. Today, with an array of options to choose from, it is much easier to find a hit and not a miss.

IT'S ALL ABOUT THAT **BASE**

UNDER TONES

When it comes to selecting the right shade of foundation, it is very important to pay attention to your skin's undertones. Just like when picking the right shade of red lipstick (which I'll share a little later), there are three types of undertones: warm, neutral, and cool.

WARM UNDERTONES
Peach, Yellow or Golden
Yellow or Peach Based

COOL UNDERTONES
Pink, Red, or Blue
Neutral or Pink Based

If you have NEUTRAL UNDERTONES, your skin will have a mixture of these colors.

• • • • • • • • • • • • • •

FIND YOUR UNDERTONE

A general guide (this is not set in stone) to find your undertone is to look at your wrist and check the color of your veins in natural light.

Green Veins = Warm
Blue Veins = Cool
Green/Blue Veins = Neutral

YOU CAN ALSO ANSWER THIS QUESTION:
When you tan do you?

Tan easily and don't burn easily.
(warm)

Burn easily and tan a little or not at all.
(cool)

QUICK BEAUTY TIP
Although I prefer to use a sponge, you will save money on liquid foundation by applying it with a brush. Sponges are porous and absorbs much of your foundation. It's also best to use a foundation brush made with synthetic hairs, which are nonabsorbent and allows for a more even coverage.

KEY WORDS
When you are shopping for foundation, there are a few key words that will give you some idea if the color has a warm, neutral, or cool undertone. Remember, these are just guidlines and will vary.

WARM
Golden, Sand, Honey, Bronze, Cream

• • • • • • • • • • • • • •

COOL
Buff, Beige, Nude, Bare

• • • • • • • • • • • • • •

NEUTRAL
Tan, Beige, Nude

TINTED MOISTURIZER
Create your own tinted moisturizer by mixing one part liquid foundation and one to two parts moisturizer, depending on how sheer you want your coverage.

IT'S ALL ABOUT THAT **BASE**

MINIMIZE PORES

For women with huge pores or acne prone skin, pores can appear larger and more prominent when you apply foundation. To eliminate the appearance of large pores, use a stippling brush and buff your foundation in a circular motion (both clockwise and counter-clockwise). When using this technique don't use too much foundation (apply foundation to skin first) in order to maintain a realistic finish. If you have dry skin, exfoliate first as this technique may cause micro-exfoliation.

Apply foundation in an outward direction (not down), being sure to blend into the hairline and neck.

TAKE NOTE: You can also use an eyeshadow brush, that is similar in shape and has soft synthetic hairs.

For large pores buff in clockwise and counter clockwise.

STIPPLING BRUSH

AVOID A MID-DAY MELTDOWN

Your makeup starts to go south in the middle of the day because of that thing called oil. It's your foundation's worste enemy, but your pores' best friend. Note the tips listed below to help you dodge your next mid-day meltdown.

-

Blot away excess oils after applying moisturizer and again after applying foundation with blotting paper or a thick tissue, then apply powder.

-

Use a mattifier gel (can be applied under or over foundation to achieve a longer lasting, shine free finish). This is what I like to use when I'm doing an on-camera shoot.

-

When you start to look shiny, blot away excess oils first, then lightly dust face with powder. If you don't blot away excess oils first, you will be left with a cakey finish.

A FOUNDATION MISTAKE EVEN MAKEUP ARTISTS MAKE

You've got 99 problems, and getting your foundation to last is probably one. Funny thing is, even some makeup artists never thought to consider this tip.

The simple answer to this complicated problem very well may be your primer. But here's the catcher: It's not the primer itself, but the type of primer.

As you may know, primer is a base for your foundation. It helps make the foundation last longer and allows for a smoother application.

Using the right type of primer under your foundation is just as important as using the proper foundation formula for your skin type.

If your foundation is water based, then you will need to use a water based primer. If you are using foundation that has a silicone base, then you will need to use a silicone based primer.

Just like oil and water don't mix, different base products don't mix and will in turn reduce the wear of your makeup.

Here's what I want you to do: Look at the ingredients label on your foundation and on your primer and see if the first three to five ingredients are similar. Look to see if these first ingredients say water, oil, or silicone. If they don't match up, then you are using the wrong primer.

If you currently don't use a primer, be sure to purchase one that is formulated to pair with your foundation.

three MOVES
TO THE PERFECT FOUNDATION

Honestly, between figuring out your undertones, and picking the right shade of foundation on top of which foundation formula to use, the odds are already stacked against you. Well, my love, here are a few pointers to help stack the odds in your favor.

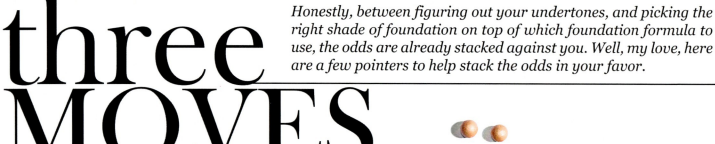

2 THE RIGHT STUFF
Your skin type will dictate what type of foundation formula you should be wearing. Women with **sensitive skin** should look for water based liquid foundations, tinted moisturizer, mousse, and mineral powder foundation. If you have **dry skin**, you should use a moisturizing liquid foundation, tinted moisturizer, or a mousse. **Normal skin** can use all formulations of foundation, including all liquids, tinted moisturizers, mousse, crème, cream to powder, and powders. If you have **oily skin**, choose an oil free liquid foundation, mineral foundation, or mousse to help control shine.

1 PRIME TIME
The first step to any flawless foundation application is to start with the perfect base. A primer helps make your foundation last longer and allows for a smoother application. To accommodate different skin types, primers can be purchased in gel, cream, and powder formulas.

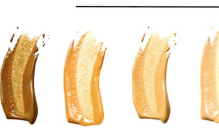

3 TONE UP
When selecting your foundation, pay close attention to your undertones. Most women tend to have yellow undertones; darker skin tones as they relate to women of color may have more red undertones; paler skin may have pink undertones; and medium or olive skin tones will usually have yellow undertones.

THE BEAUTY DIARY EDITORIAL EDITION

the top 5 FOUNDATION MISTAKES

True, we all want flawless looking skin. But before you purchase your next bottle of foundation, you need to know the true mastery of smoother looking skin starts with knowing a few important things. Read on to see if you need to check yo' self on any of these five common mistakes.

2 ONLY USING ONE SHADE OF FOUNDATION

Women of color typically have different tones throughout their skin, making their skin appear lighter in the center of their face and darker around the edges. If you find that using a darker shade foundation all over your face makes you look artificial, simply use a lighter shade in the center of your face and blend into the darker shade.

4 NOT APPLYING FOUNDATION TO YOUR NECK

When you apply foundation, remember to blend into your neck for a more natural finish. If you choose the correct shade of foundation, this will result in a seamless blend. Not doing so will leave a distinct line and make you look like you are wearing a mask.

1 NOT PROPERLY TESTING YOUR FOUNDATION

When selecting the right shade of foundation, always test in natural light. Test about three to four shades that are close to your complexion on your jawline. Make sure the color you choose matches the color of your neck and is not too red, pink, or yellow. The correct color will disappear on your face. To make sure you have selected the right color, take a mirror and go outside to see how it looks in natural light. You may be surprised how it really looks.

3 APPLYING CONCEALER THE WRONG WAY

When applying your concealer, most would argue that you should apply your foundation first, to avoid rubbing away your concealer when you apply your foundation. Although sometimes I do prefer applying my foundation first (only because I may use foundation as a sheer base), your concealer will pretty much stay put if you apply both your concealer and foundation in a tapping motion (making sure to blend well) with your wet sponge, a dry brush, or with your fingertips, instead of a swiping motion, which will only move the product around. Also, make sure the concealer you use around your eye area is creamy and not dry.

5 NOT APPLYING POWDER PROPERLY

Press your loose powder into your skin with a powder brush or makeup puff using a blotting motion. Buffing or swiping your powder will shift your foundation, as opposed to setting it in place.

If you are faced with one or more of these popular foundation mistakes, don't become overwhelmed. I encourage you to tackle one problem at a time. Start with the first tip. Grab your current shade and test your foundation. Does it match up? If yes, then move on to step two. If not, it's time to purchase a new shade. Remember, if your foundation shade is wrong, the other tips won't really matter.

THE BEAUTY DIARY EDITORIAL EDITION

POWDER FORMULAS

Loose/Translucent powder comes in a jar and has a light, finer consistency. It yields lightweight coverage and can even be used as a sheer foundation.

Pressed powder is sold in a compact and provides a more opaque coverage. It contains ingredients like silicones and waxes so over applying will result in a cakey finish.

Setting powder is the powder I mentioned above. It's basic powder you use to set your foundation and concealer, and to eliminate shine. It can be tinted to match your skin or translucent.

Finishing powder is used after setting powder to soften up any fine lines, pores, and wrinkles on flash cameras, like an HD powder. As a novice I would stay clear from using this product. If not used right you will end up with white streaks and patches on your face that are only visible on camera.

THE APPLICATION

You can set your foundation by using a powder brush or a velour or circular sponge. If using a brush, dip into the powder, tap off any excess powder, and press the brush into the skin using a rolling motion. Do not swipe the brush across your face as this will move your foundation and may reveal any imperfections you have tried to cover. When using a sponge, dip it into the powder, rub the powder into the sponge, and tap off excess. Press the sponge into the skin.

LOOSE & TRANSLUCENT POWDER

PRESSED POWDER

VELOUR SPONGE

GET SET!
THE ULTIMATE POWER OF
POWDER

Powder is a key step in wearing and setting your makeup. It helps keep your concealer and foundation in place. If you get this wrong, not only was finding the right shade of foundation a waste of time, but your final look will also end up looking fake.

QUICK BEAUTY TIP

Be sure to powder your neck as well. This will ensure the light reflects evenly when taking pictures and avoids a lighter "ghost" like face.

THE BEAUTY DIARY   EDITORIAL EDITION

GET SET! THE ULTIMATE POWER OF POWDER

Bronze Powder is a great alternative to tanning to achieve sun-kissed skin. This powder should be applied with a big fluffy brush around the hairline, under the cheekbone, your jawline, and neck. For a quick and easy way to apply bronzer, think of creating a big number 3 or two letter "C's" on your face. Finish look with a warm apricot or rosy blush.

Iridescent Powder is a finely milled mixture of mica and pigments which can be used if you desire a shimmery look. It can also be mixed into other products like moisturizers and foundations for an all over glow.

SOFT HIGHLIGHTS

After you apply foundation and concealer, and set your foundation, applying extra powder down the bridge of your nose, under the eyes, and under your bottom lip will yield soft highlights in these area, making for a nice everyday contour. Be sure to dust away and blend any excess powder once you finish applying your makeup.

TAKE NOTE:

#1
the same shade
Your powder should be as close to your natural complexion as possible. Avoid powders that are too red and too light.

#2
shake it off
Shake off excess powder before applying to avoid an uneven and overdone application.

#3
silky smooth
A good quality powder will feel silky and light.

#4
blot first
Remember, don't use your pressed powder as your go-to for minimizing and eliminating shine. Use blotting paper or tissue to blot away oils. Over application of powder will make you look cakey.

#5
skip the powder
If you use a cream-to-powder foundation, you can skip the loose powder as it already sets to a powdery finish.

#6
home & travel
To minimize the mess, use your loose powder at home and your pressed powder on the go.

#7
powder first
Apply powder before applying a powder based blush to prevent the oils in your skin from grabbing the color and leaving a blotchy finish.

THE BEAUTY DIARY · EDITORIAL EDITION

GLOWING RADIANT SKIN

There are different ways to achieve glowing looking skin, but I find this method to be the best, most straightforward approach. I think this look is more authentic when worn on a bright sunny day, and not when it's raining or gloomy. To successfully create this look, stay away from any products with a matte finish (excluding the eye area) and products that say "sparkly" or "glittery," as the particles in these products are too big and will not result in a natural looking glow.

MOISTURIZER & PRIMER
Use a moisturizer that is best for your skin type. Apply a luminous primer on the face and a waterproof eyeshadow primer on your eyelids.

FOUNDATION
Apply the foundation to your face and blend with a brush into the neck. For an all over glow, sometimes I like to add a little liquid illuminator with my foundation.

CONCEALER
Next, apply concealer to the under eye area and inner corners of the eyes with a sponge using a patting motion to conceal imperfections.

HIGHLIGHT
Using a blender sponge, lightly pat on an illuminator or glowing highlighter on the upper cheek bones (this should be the area that you highlight the most). For an extra glow, apply to the center of your forehead, down the bridge of your nose (but only where your nose dips and the tip of your nose), and your cupid's bow.

POWDER
Lightly set with powder using a powder brush. Do not over apply because you want to retain that glowing finish. You can also use a shimmery powder, but make sure the brand has designed it as part of its "dewy" or "glow" collection. This will help you avoid selecting a shimmery powder that will not result in a natural looking finish. Be sure to blend well to avoid streaks.

BRONZER
Dust a soft layer of bronzer around the hairline, the hollows of your cheeks, your jawline, and your neck. (See previous page for details.)

BLUSH
To add a pop of color to your skin, apply a peachy or apricot blush for warmer skin tones and a soft pink for lighter skin tones.

MAKEUP
Keep your look fresh with soft shimmery eye shadows and natural lip color like soft nude pink, peach, or soft rose. Line the waterline part of your eyes with a soft cream liner. Curl lashes and apply mascara to make the eyes pop. Don't go over the top as it should look like something you would wear to the beach. Finish with setting spray.

GLOWING RADIANT SKIN

You can clearly see that a glittery powder was applied to her chest. Notice how the glow on her face appears more natural compared to the larger sparkles on her chest.

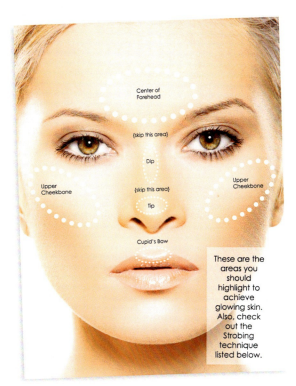

These are the areas you should highlight to achieve glowing skin. Also, check out the Strobing technique listed below.

STROBING
A.K.A HIGHLIGHTING WITHOUT CONTOURING

Don't get hung up on the name. Basically you just blend a small amount of highlighting cream, illuminator, or bronze iridescent powder on the tops of your cheekbones.

TAKE NOTE...

To create a natural, even appearance, be sure to add some highlights to your neck and chest areas too.

-

Avoid products that have a pink tint as it can make darker skin appear ashy.

-

If you have oily skin, you may want to simply highlight the upper cheek area and cupid's bow to minimize mid-day shine.

PRIME
If you have oily skin, before applying foundation apply a matte primer to your T-zone and upper lip area to help minimize shine.

BRONZING
To enhance your highlights add a light dusting of bronzer, not to contour but to add warmth to the skin.

FAN BRUSH
When highlighting, remember that a little goes a long way. Start with a very tiny amount and apply as needed.

THE BEAUTY DIARY EDITORIAL EDITION

Camouflage That
Double Chin!

Unless you are skilled at blending your makeup, I caution you to use this technique only for pictures and evening events. In addition, if your double chin hangs considerably low (what some refer to as a turkey neck), girlfriend, you should keep it movin' – this tip ain't for you.

Color Theory:
The lighter something is, the bigger it will appear. The darker something is, the smaller it will appear. Shading helps make an area fade away.

1. PICK A SHADE
Select a foundation a few shades darker than your skin tone.

5. SET WITH POWDER
Set with a darker shade of powder using a sponge to press the powder into the skin.

2. SHAPE IT OUT
Using a foundation brush or sponge, create a triangle shape under the bottom of your chin toward your jawline, and fill in.

3. BLEND IT OUT
Blend into the neck area, blending into the hollow areas of your neck that frame the Adam's Apple.

4. DEFINE
For a more defined jawline, create an "L" shape starting in front of the ear and lining your jawline and back toward the ear.

blushing

You may think applying blush and picking the right formula can be tricky, but it doesn't have to be if you don't overthink it. Simply pick the formula that suits your fancy then apply to your cheeks using these simple tips.

which formula?

Powder
Powder blush is typically suitable for all skin types, especially oily skin. Mostly sold as a pressed powder, you may also find it in a mineral loose powder form. I think they are the easiest to apply and blend. Always tap off excess powder before applying, and to achieve a streak free application, be sure to apply loose powder first so the blush does not absorb the excess oils on the skin.

Gel, Creams, Tints and Stains
Suitable for all skin types as well, and ideal if you have drier skin. For the most part, the only difference between these types of blushes are the packaging and the texture. Just like foundations and concealers, cream blushes come in a stick or pot, while the others have a more liquid consistency and come in a tube with a pump or a bottle. Some may argue these formulas are longer lasting, but they are more difficult to apply and blend, and can leave an unnatural finish. Apply your cream blush with a brush or with your fingers. For gels, tints and stains, apply two small drops to your cheeks and blend using your fingers.

the application

Depending on your face shape, there are different application techniques you can use to apply blush, but to keep things simple, blush always looks best when applied to the cheekbone.

To find your cheekbone, follow the line from the top part of your ear to your nose. Use the outer part of your pupil as a starting point and apply blush with a light hand in a circular motion up toward your ear.

quick tips

When applying your blush, don't smile as it can create fine lines. If you are a mature woman, your cheeks may not be as high once you stop smiling and the application placement will be too low.

For blush that lasts, use two shades – a natural shade across your cheekbones and a brighter shade applied just on the apples of your cheeks.

THE BEAUTY DIARY 55 EDITORIAL EDITION

cheeks that POP!

It can be a difficult undertaking to try and figure out what the best color blush is for your skin tone. A color that is too light will wash out your complexion and make you look grossly ashen, while anything too dark will leave your makeup looking completely unnatural. I want to save you from having to swatch all those pretty color blushes so here's a guide for choosing the best color blush.

BROWN

FUCHSIA

TANGERINE

DARK SKIN TONE

Deep and warm shades of fuchsia, brown, and tangerine are the most ideal blush colors for darker beauties. For warmer-colored skin tones, try a deep fuchsia, which will immediately add radiance to your complexion. If your skin tone tends to be cooler, try a blush with orange undertones.

ROSY PINK

WARM MAUVE

DEEP PEACH

MEDIUM & OLIVE SKIN TONE

The best color options are rich, deep colors like a rosy pink, warm mauve, and deep peach. A warm mauve (cross-breed between a pink and purple) looks incredible for olive skin tones that are on the cooler side, and as for those who have a warmer complexion, opt for a rose hue that will help accentuate your lovely warm undertones.

THE BEAUTY DIARY *58* EDITORIAL EDITION

SOFT PINK

APRICOTS

PEACH

PEACHY KEEN FOR FAIR & ANY SKIN TONE

The lovely shades of peaches and apricots, which can add a natural sun-kissed glow to just about any complexion.

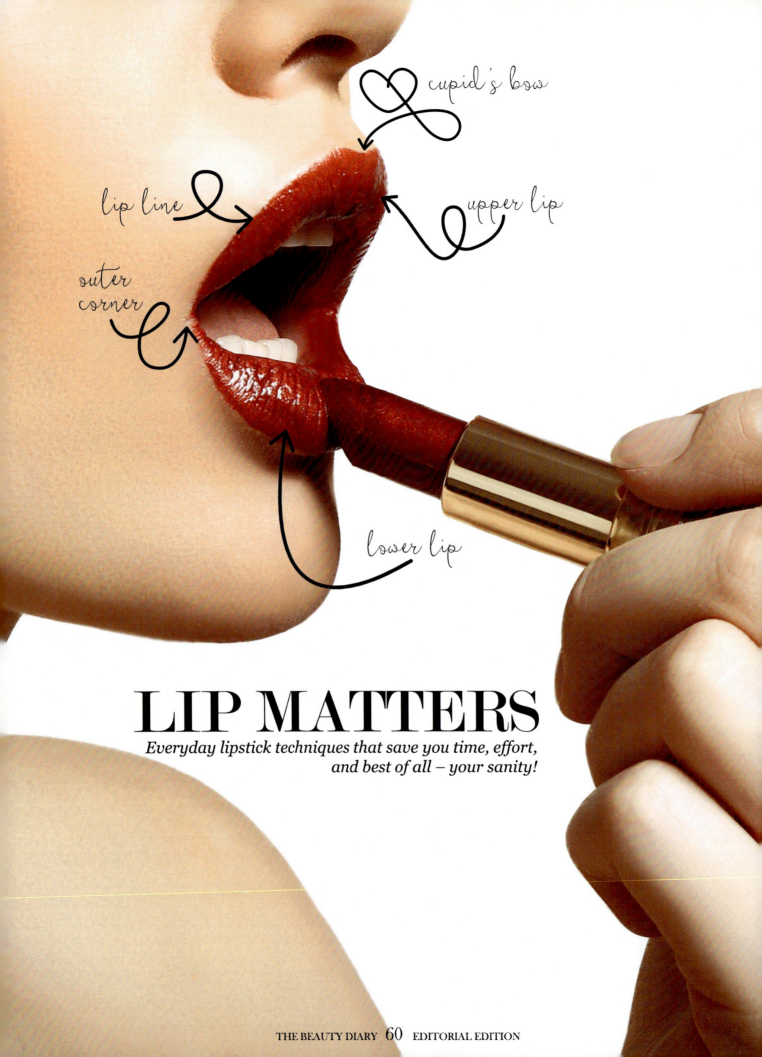

LIP MATTERS
Everyday lipstick techniques that save you time, effort, and best of all – your sanity!

BLEND THE LINE Use your lip brush or your finger, or simply rub your lips together to blend out your lip liner before applying lip color. This eliminates a harsh line and creates a gradient effect for a softer, more natural look.

INTENSIFY
YOUR LIP COLOR

Apply lip primer (or a little concealer or foundation) to help keep lip color true and to help keep your lipstick from bleeding.

CUPID'S BOW

Draw an "X" in the center of your upper lip to define your Cupid's bow.

QUICK BEAUTY TIPS

Make your lip color last by lining and filling in your lips with your lip liner before applying color.

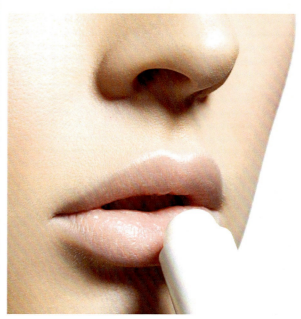

MAKE IT SOFT Moisturize your lips right after brushing your teeth. This allows the balm time to penetrate before you apply your lip color. Be sure to blot off excess moisturizer before applying lip color.

give it the FINGER

An oldie but goodie: slide your finger between your lips to prevent color from getting on your teeth. Many of you know this tip, but few of you use it.

BEST way to BLOT

Apply lip color then blot by pressing the tissue on the lips. Placing the tissue between your lips makes for an uneven wear.

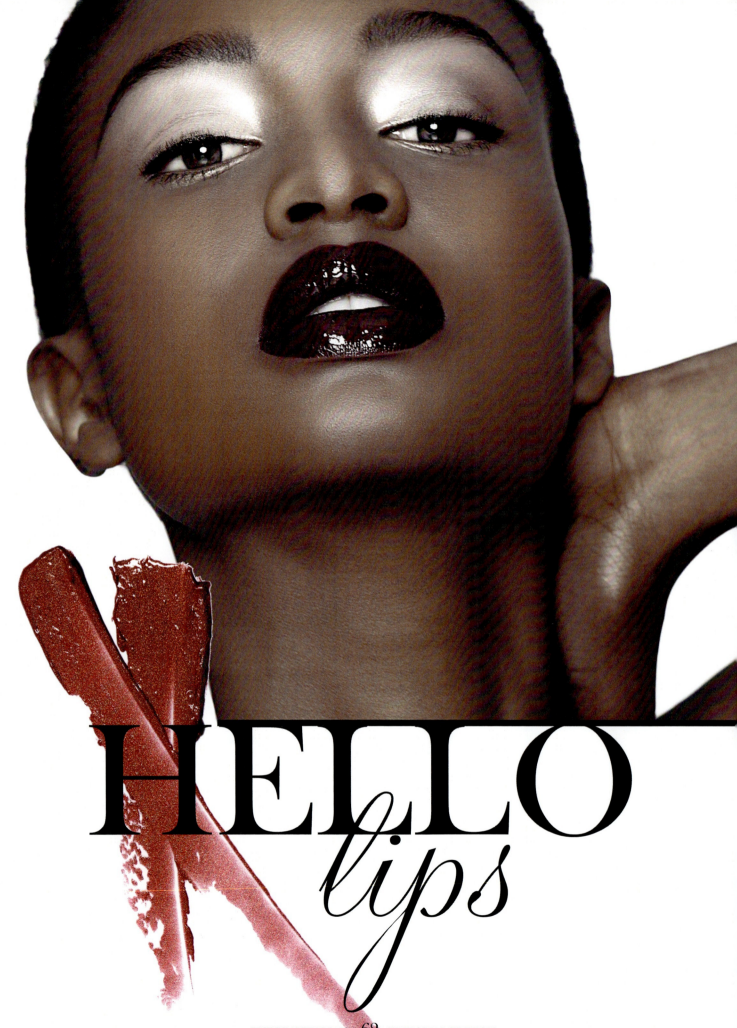

HELLO *lips*

STEP 1
Start with well moisturized lips.

STEP 2
Apply a lip primer to help keep your lip color true and keep it from bleeding.

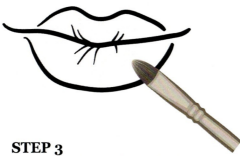

STEP 3
Define the shape of your lips by using your desired lip liner pencil.

(Depending on how dark my lip liner is, I like to rub my lips together to help blend out the lip liner, which helps eliminate obvious lines.)

STEP 4
Using a lip brush, fill in your lips with color up to your lip line.

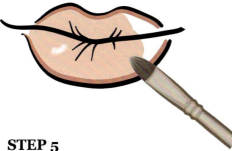

STEP 5
Blot with tissue to remove excess oils, then reapply lip color for a longer lasting wear.

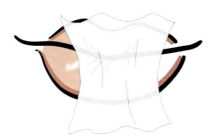

Knowing how to apply your lipstick properly can turn out to be the best thing ever, especially for those days when you're not interested in wearing a full face.

POPULAR LIP COLOR FORMULAS

Cream
moisturizing and makes lips look smoother

Matte
bold and eye catching

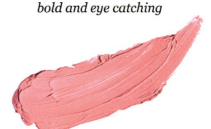

Sheer
glides on easily and shows fewer application flaws

Shiny
makes lips look fuller

RED LINER
To intensify color and for a more defined lip, use a red lip liner to outline lips and fill in lips.

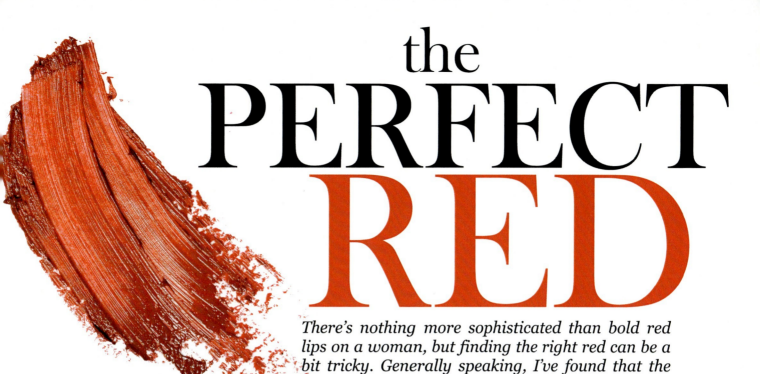

the PERFECT RED

There's nothing more sophisticated than bold red lips on a woman, but finding the right red can be a bit tricky. Generally speaking, I've found that the search for the perfect red lips is not just based on your skin tone, but also your undertone.

ONE MAJOR POINT TO NOTE:
Red lipstick comes in three hues: Orange/Red (warm), Neutral/Red (neutral), and Blue/Red (cool). Turn to page 43 for tips on how to find your undertone.

FAIR
(cool)
Don't be afraid to go bold; the pink undertones in fair skin will not only contrast nicely against vibrant blue-based cherry reds, but will also make your teeth look whiter.

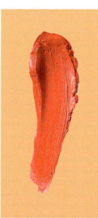

MEDIUM
(cool)
A pinkish-red is best suited for medium-light complexions that are cooler.

DARK
(cool)
When selecting a red for a darker skin with cool undertones, go with a blue-based berry red.

FAIR
(warm)
If you are a fair skin woman with warm undertones, opt for a deep orange-red.

MEDIUM
(warm)
A vivid, fiery red will wonderfully complement warm complexions.

DARK
(warm)
Orange-based reds will complement the warmth of dark skin beauties. A deep merlot will go nicely too.

{ *I would go as far as saying to try a range of reds (from light to dark shades) that complement your skins warm, neutral, or cool undertones.* }

THE BEAUTY DIARY — EDITORIAL EDITION

Here's the kicker: If you have dry lips, you may need to give yourself a few days to prep your lips before rocking a matte lip.

A MATTE MADE IN HEAVEN

Get your matte lipstick to go on smoothly and wear it well.

SCRUB-A-DUB
Matte lip color can be waxing and very drying, so it's vital that you start with a well-exfoliated lip and remove dead skin to avoid a cakey finish. Apply a coat of petroleum jelly and let it sit for 15 minutes, then rub dry skin away with a warm washcloth. Or use a gentle lip scrub and massage with your finger.

KEEP THEM HYDRATED
A great matte lip does not equal dry. Apply a thin layer of lip moisturizer first, and be sure to blot off excess moisturizer before applying lip color.

GET PRIMED
Since your lips aren't an even shade, create an even base for a more vivid color and give your matte shade staying power by applying a lip primer before applying lip liner and lipstick.

MAKE IT PRECISE
Matte lipstick is super pigmented so uneven lines will surely be seen. Apply your color straight from the tube for a smoother application, then tidy up your outline with a matching lip liner. Be sure to fill in your lips halfway with the lip liner for a more blended finish.

A CLEAN FINISH
For a perfect finish, clean up around the edges of your lips with a skin-tone foundation or powder for an extra clean line.

QUICK BEAUTY TIP

A MATTE SUBSTITUTE
If you don't have a matte lipstick opt for a lip liner.

—

TURN IT MATTE
Turn your cream lipstick in matte finish by applying a liberal amount of translucent powder to eliminate the shine. Just note the powder will lighten up the color of your lipstick, so use a darker lip liner before applying your lip color.

—

GET IT OFF
For stubborn lip color apply petroleum jelly to your lips and wipe away with a tissue.

1
BUFF & BALM
No lip color will look its best if applied over dry, chapped lips. As I mentioned before, apply a coat of petroleum jelly and let it sit for 15 minutes, then rub dry skin away with a warm washcloth. Or use a gentle lip scrub and massage with your finger. Then apply lip balm.

2
STAYING POWER
To give your lip color longer wear, start by applying a lip primer, then line your lips and fill in your lips with a lip liner.

3
DODGE THE DARK
Apply lip color as usual but try to stay away from darker colors as they will make your lip appear smaller.

4
LINE & DEFINE
Next, outline your lips with a concealer to make your pout more defined.

5
HIGHLIGHT
Give your lips a little oomph and make them look fuller by highlighting. Apply a little gloss or highlighter in the center of your top and bottom lip. It's the same principle you use when you highlight and contour your face. The darker shade makes areas recede and the lighter shade brings the areas forward.

6
CUPID'S BOW
If your lips are your best asset, enhance your Cupid's bow with a highlighter.

something to POUT about

Your lips may not be the biggest, and that's cool. But it doesn't mean you can't give them a little oomph and make them stand out.

WHAT YOU'LL NEED:
1. Lipstick (any shade)
2. Lip liner (one that compliments your lipstick)
3. Stick Concealer/Foundation
4. Clear Lip Gloss (optional)

Ombré
giving shade in 3 steps

Step #1
Apply your lip liner to outline your lips and fill in the corners of your mouth, blending slightly inward. Then gently rub lips together, or blend with a lip brush, to remove any harsh lines.

Step #2
Apply your lipstick and gently rub your lips together to blend lip liner and lipstick.

Step #3
With your finger, rub some concealer on your finger and gently tap onto the center of your top and bottom lips, then press your lips together (do not rub them together, but press them) to blend out concealer. Apply more if needed or until you reach the desired look.

Finsh with lip gloss if desired.

Ombré, which literally means "shade" in French, is the gradual blending of one color hue to another from light to dark. Artists have been using this technique forever and it usually requires a lot of blending. Although this look has techniques similar to some of the techniques I shared on how to get a fuller pout, here I share with you how to achieve the ombré look in three easy steps.

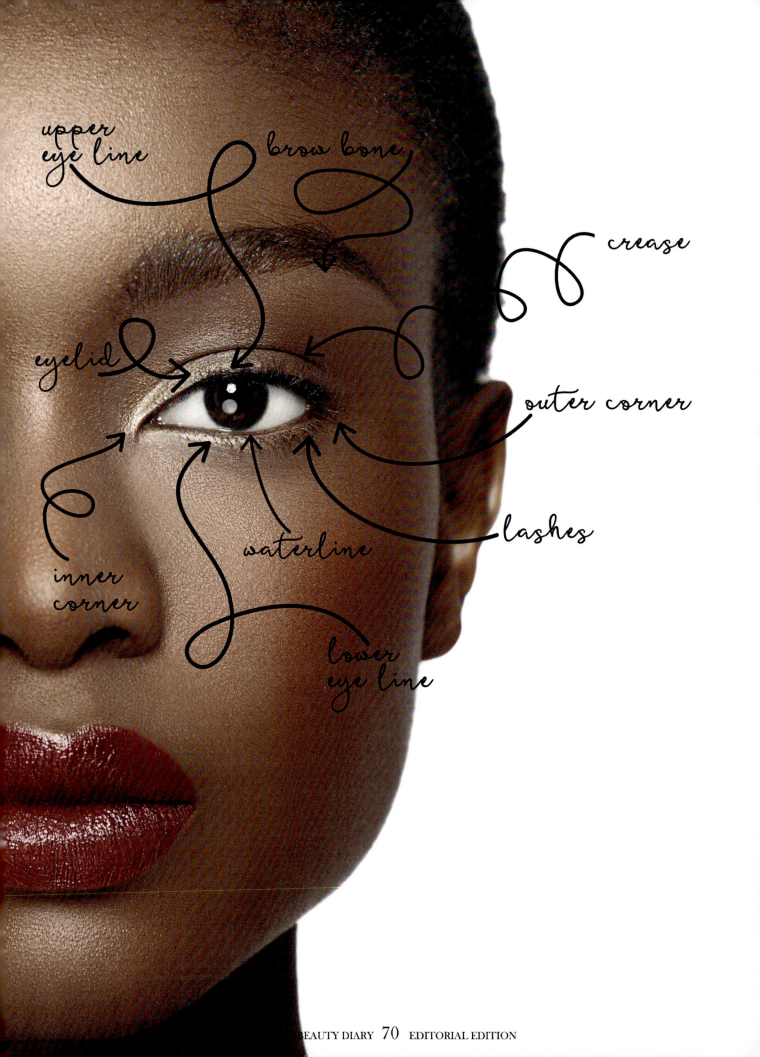

THE MISSING STEP TO THICKER LOOKING LASHES

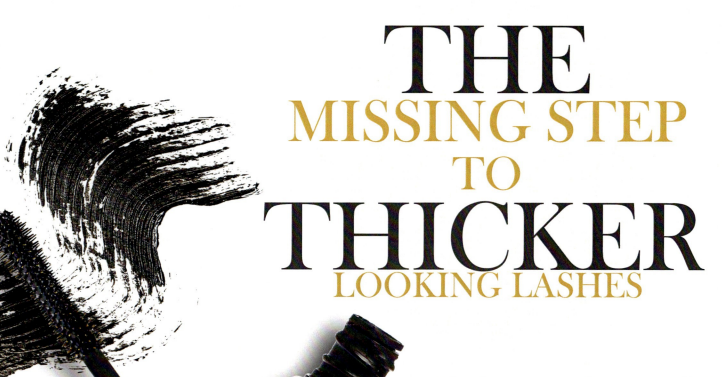

When it comes to wearing mascara, this is by no means your first rodeo. So you already know the key to thick, natural looking lashes isn't piling on layers and layers of mascara.

But what you haven't figured out is how you can get thicker looking lashes without adding false lashes into your makeup routine.

This simple technique I'm about to share will have you saying, "Seriously, why didn't I think of that?"

If you have fine or short lashes, the solution is to apply mascara on both sides of your lashes. Yup, that's it. So here's what you do:

Remove excess product from the mascara wand by wiping the wand with a tissue. It may seem wasteful, but too much mascara leads to clumps, and there's nothing natural looking about that.

Apply a very small amount of waterproof mascara to the back of your lashes first. Start at the base of your lashes and shake from side-to-side straight through the tips of the lashes.

Next, apply mascara to the front of your lashes using the same side-to-side motion. Add an additional coat of mascara if desired. Apply mascara to your bottom lashes.

Once completely dry, curl your top lashes with an eyelash curler.

FIVE STEPS TO... BOMBSHELL LASHES

If applying mascara resulted in full, voluminous lashes like in the commercials, you'd sport long, luxurious eyelashes while cooking Sunday brunch. But since that ain't the case, and due to the various technical difficulties caused by the lack of technique, you end up with clumpy lashes instead of lashes that look fuller and flawless. So what to do? Simply use these five steps to leave your eyelashes clump free and looking like false lashes.

STEP 1 — IT'S ALL ABOUT THE MASCARA
To get lashes to stay longer and to minimize product transfer, use Waterproof Mascara.

STEP 2 — WIPE IT AWAY
Remove excess product from the mascara wand by wiping the wand with a tissue. Yes, it may seem wasteful but too much mascara leads to clumps.

STEP 3 — SQUEEZE & CURL
Curl your lashes with an eyelash curler. Start from the base and work your way up the lash to achieve a gradual curl. Squeeze and hold, ideally for five seconds, as you work your way up.

STEP 4 — A LITTLE GOES A LONG WAY
Apply a very, very small amount of waterproof mascara. Start at the base of your lash and shake from side-to-side straight through the tips of the lashes. If you have fine or short lashes, be sure to apply mascara on both sides of your lashes.

STEP 5 — CURL & RE-APPLY
Once the mascara is dry, curl your lashes again using the same technique. Apply additional coats of mascara as desired, but in very small amounts each time. Use a lash comb to separate lashes and to remove any excess mascara.

BONUS TIPS:
- Do not apply mascara to bottom lashes if they are very sparse — you are just making it more noticeable.
- If you tend to get mascara transfer from your lashes, do not apply mascara to the tips.
- If you get mascara on your skin, to avoid it smearing, wait until it dries before removing.

eyelash comb

eyelash curler

THE BEAUTY DIARY — EDITORIAL EDITION

rocking
LASHES WITH GLASSES

You might not have been born with 20/20 vision, but that doesn't mean wearing glasses should stop you from batting a full set of luscious lashes. If you've always wanted the fun, flirty, behind-the-glasses lashes, here are some helpful tips to consider.

1. ADD VOLUME
If you're looking to add more volume to your dense lashes, consider opting for individual lashes which will help fill in the spaces of your natural lashes and give you more volume without having them collide against your glasses.

2. CURLS AT THE END
The best eye lash look for eyeglass wearers is lashes that look natural, but with a touch of length? Choose falsies that have a slight wisp or curl at the outer end of the lashes, to prevent them from rubbing against your lens.

3. JUST AN ACCENT
Accent lashes are increasingly popular if you are after a more natural look. Simply apply the accent lashes to the outer corners of your eyes for just a touch of natural glamour.

4. CURL EM'
If you already have a pair of false eye lashes that are just too long, – reach for an eyelash curler and curl those lashes inwards to prevent them from hitting your lens. Although this step is not my go to, be sure to curl close to the lash line to create a natural looking curl.

Lash
wear & care

I like to think that I'm a bona fide pro when it comes to applying lashes, but when it comes to applying lashes on myself, even I sometimes don't come with my "A" game. Which is why I couldn't wait to share some tips on lash application and a simple technique to applying false lashes if you're one of those who just can't seem to get it right.

PREP TIP:
Before applying your lashes, line your eyes, curl your lashes, and apply a thin coat of mascara to your own lashes for a more seamless blend. I also recommend using a black or dark color lash glue, which will help define your eyes.

REMOVAL

Step 5
Dab oil-free makeup remover on a cotton swab {or use a makeup wipe} and wipe along the band of the lashes. Wait about 15 seconds for the glue to dissolve. Repeat as needed.

Step 6
Remove lashes by gently pulling from the outer corner of the eyes. Lashes should come off eyes effortlessly. Never tug on the hairs or individual strands.

Step 7
Carefully peel {with your fingertips or tweezers} or wipe off remnants of lash glue from the lash band with a moist cotton swab or makeup wipe.

Step 8
To keep your lashes in perfect condition, store your lashes in the original container after each use, to help retain their shape and to protect from dust.

CARE

Step 9
Use an eyelash curler to curl your natural lashes. NEVER curl your false lashes because it will not result in a natural shape curl.

Step 10
Use any lash glue designed for use with strip lashes. DO NOT use lash glue designed for use with individual lashes.

Step 11
Do not soak or clean your lashes with water or other chemicals. This will ruin the natural curl and quality and will shorten the lifespan of the lashes. If your lashes become dusty, gently rub lashes with a dry cotton swab.

Never coat lashes with mascara or other products.

APPLICATION

Step 1
Using tweezers, gently remove lashes from the tray by the outer edge of the lash band. Never tug on the hairs or individual strands.

Step 2
Check eyelash fit by aligning it with your natural lash line. Trim away excess from the outer edges only.

Step 3
Apply a thin coat of adhesive to the lash band, wait 30 seconds, or until glue becomes tacky.

Step 4
Using your fingers or a pair of tweezers, apply to eyelid as close to natural lash line as possible. Secure inner and outer corners by pushing down to the corners of your eyes.

QUICK BEAUTY TIP

First and foremost, to keep lashes looking natural opt for short to medium length lashes. Lashes that are too long scream "fake" and that defeats the point.

Often-times, lining up your false lashes can be a bit tricky. When you go to attach one end, the other end may pop up or attach itself a little too high. When I apply lashes on myself, I've found cutting my lashes in half and then applying them makes for a much easier application.

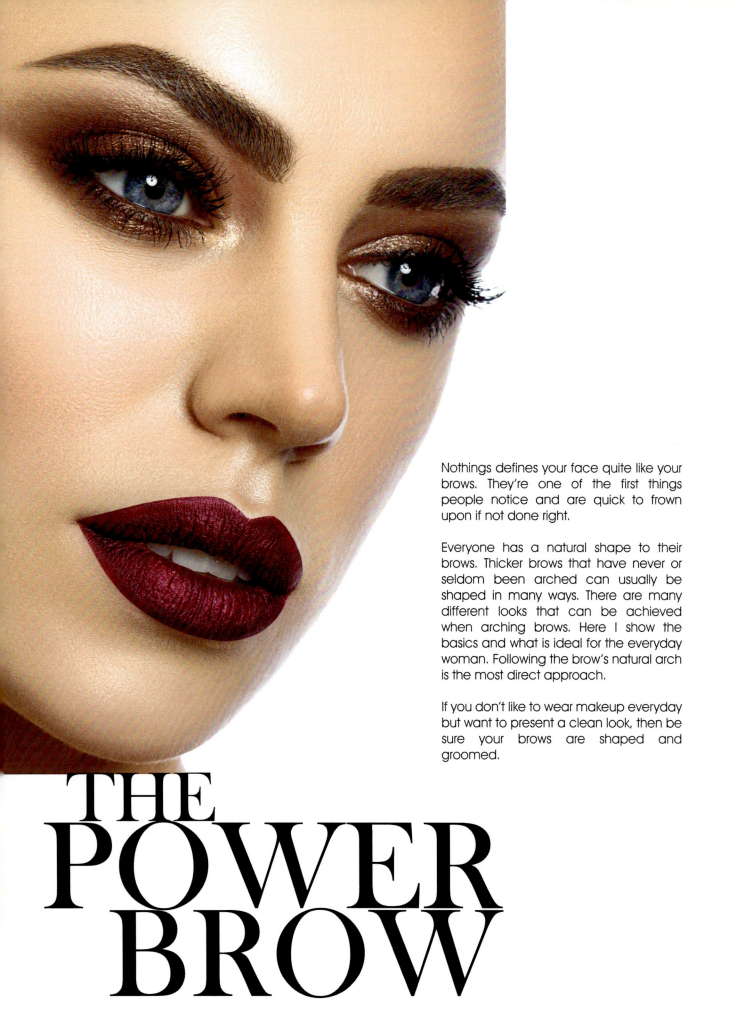

Nothings defines your face quite like your brows. They're one of the first things people notice and are quick to frown upon if not done right.

Everyone has a natural shape to their brows. Thicker brows that have never or seldom been arched can usually be shaped in many ways. There are many different looks that can be achieved when arching brows. Here I show the basics and what is ideal for the everyday woman. Following the brow's natural arch is the most direct approach.

If you don't like to wear makeup everyday but want to present a clean look, then be sure your brows are shaped and groomed.

THE POWER BROW

STEP 1
You should first determine where your brows will begin, end, and arch. Consider these shaping points as a guide. Point 1 should line up with the inner part of your eyes (if you have wide set eyes feel free to move your starting point further in so your brows can appear closer together. Just determine what you feel more comfortable with). Point 2 should line up with the outer part of the pupil. Shaping point 3 should line up with and not pass the outer part of your eyes.

STEP 2
For the natural shape of your brow, pay close attention to the curve on the top of the brow.

STEP 3
Using this natural shape as a guide, mimic the same shape along the bottom of your brow by removing the most obvious hairs.

STEP 4
Mark hairs you want to remove with a white or nude eyeliner pencil or concealer. If you don't have a steady hand, feel free to use an eyebrow template as a guide. This can be purchased at your local beauty supply store.

STEP 5
Pluck hairs in the direction they have grown. This technique is less painful. For hairs at the top of the brow, I usually just trim them if they fall in line with the natural arch.

STEP 6
My favorite way to fill in sparse brows is by using a brow powder or a brown or black powder eyeshadow with a soft eyeliner brush. The powder yields a soft, natural looking finish and the liner brush, used at an angle, makes application more precise.

With an ample amount on powder on the brush (but not too much) start at the inner part of the brow and line under the brow first. Now line the top part of the brow. Using the remaining powder on the brush, fill in brows. Add additional powder if needed.

(If using the powder and brush technique seems to be more challenging, use a brow pencil. However, to avoid the hard, waxy look a pencil usually creates, fill in the brows lightly with the pencil and brush through brows with a brow brush. Be sure to follow up with a light dusting of powder to give your brows a more natural finish.)

NOTE:
Brow hairs do not grow back thicker. In most cases, constant plucking may cause individual hairs to stop growing.

KEEP BROWS IN PLACE:
To keep unruly brows in place, you can use a brow gel, clear mascara, or hairspray. When using hairspray, be sure to spray the mascara wand and not your face.

LINE *like a* PRO

LIQUID liners require a steady hand. It yields a more precise application, but leaves an inky, unnatural looking finish. Apply with provided applicator; it requires a minute or so to dry.

GEL (sometimes referred to as cake) liner is not as forgiving as a pencil although it glides on fairly easily and leaves a matte finish. It usually comes in a little pot and requires a brush to apply.

PENCIL eyeliner is easy to apply and is the most forgiving. At times it may not spread evenly, yet it yields soft rich lines, which makes it ideal for smudging.

LINE *like a* PRO

To know your eye shape is one thing; to line them is a whole other story. These tips will help you master the art of applying eyeliner, and in time you'll line like a pro.

If you make a mistake, wait until it dries then clean up with a cotton swab soaked in makeup remover. For more noticeable mistakes, swipe on a bit of concealer or foundation to achieve a cleaner finish.

To soften up the edges of a flawed eyeliner application, use a smudge brush or an angled eyeliner brush.

CONNECT THE DOTS...

There are some things you learn in school that you can actually use in real life. In this case, it's when you were in Pre-K and you learned how to connect the dots. Place dots along the eye line to use as a guide.

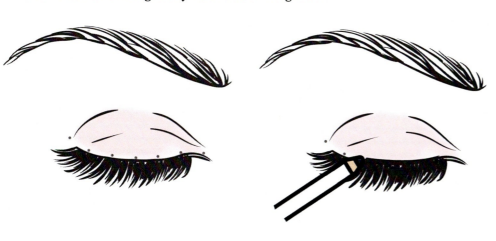

QUICK BEAUTY TIP

When applying liner, avoid pulling on the outer part of your eyes. Instead, get close to the mirror, look straight and tilt your head back, keeping your eyes open. This position will give you a better view point of your lash line.

—

Keep your application technique stable by placing your pinky on your cheek while lining your eyes.

Monolids Eye Shape

QUICK BEAUTY TIP

WHEN LINING EYES <u>NEVER</u>:

Line just the bottom eyelid. This will drag your eyes down.

Apply liquid liner on the bottom lash line as it will appear too harsh. Opt for a pencil liner instead, which you can smudge to create a softer line.

LINE *like a* PRO

Basic Eye Shape

Let me start by saying that everything ain't for everybody. With that being said, it's important to note that eyeliner's main mission is to create a thicker, darker lash line and to enhance your lashes, making them appear thicker.

Eyeliner can also give your eyes a different appearance depending on the color used. Read along for tips on how to line your eyes based on your eye shape, and how the color you apply can enhance your eyes.

WIDE SET EYES
Apply eyeliner slightly thicker, with the same thickness across the entire lash line to make the eyes appear rounder.

BASIC EYE SHAPE
This eye shape is where you can see the entire eyelid when your eyes are open, including deep set eyes. Any eyeliner application will work, but if you have a small eyelid, make sure you draw a thin line of eyeliner so it doesn't look like your entire lid is covered in liner.

If you have a larger eyelid, you can make your liner a little thick. But make sure you don't make it too think as it will start to look overworked.

This shape of eye is also great for creating a wing eyeliner.

HOODED, MONOLIDS, ALMOND EYES
These eye shapes usually end up hiding most, if not all, your eyeliner. Don't try to overcompensate by drawing super thick lines, as it won't be flattering once you close your eyes. Tightline by applying eyeliner between your lash line into your waterline. You can also line very close to your lash line, making sure to follow the natural curve of your eyes.

CLOSE SET EYES
Make the line thick on the outer corner of your eyes to help the eyes appear further apart from the center. Remember what I shared with you about shading: the lighter area always comes forward and the darker area recedes.

COLOR HIT LIST

BLACK
=
bold

GRAY
=
softly stated

BROWN
=
soft & subtle

WHITE/NUDE
=
wider & brighter

COLORS + METALLICS
=
fashionable

THE BEAUTY DIARY EDITORIAL EDITION

QUICK
BEAUTY TIP

If you are not comfortable using a liquid or gel eyeliner, use a black eyeliner pencil to draw your lines then go over it with a liquid eyeliner. When creating a wing tip, I also like to line under my eyes first. It allows to me follow the natural upward angle of the eye, which makes for a more perfect wing.

WINGING IT

This is one makeup look that seems to constantly go in and out of style. Well, never totally out, but at times just not considered trendy. This look is for those who like to walk a little more on the wild side, and who have an edgy style. It's a fun one to try if you have a steady hand and are comfortable with working with gel or liquid eyeliner. But even if you're not, there is a solution.

WHAT YOU'LL NEED:
Black Eyeliner Pencil
Black Liquid or Gel Eyeliner
Liquid Metallic Taupe Eyeshadow
Black Mascara

STEP 1
Line your top and bottom waterline and gently smudge it into your lash line.

STEP 2
In a circular motion, starting in the center of your eye, apply a liquid metallic taupe eyeshadow across your eyelid and into the crease. Blend well to eliminate any obvious lines.

STEP 3
Also, apply to the outer corner of your eye, under your lash line.

STEP 4
Next, draw a line from the outer corner of your bottom lash line, at an angle up towards your crease.

STEP 5
Start at the inner corner of your eyes and draw a line along your upper lash line and extend the line until it connects to the bottom eyeliner.

STEP 6
Apply black mascara to curled lases to finish the look.

THE BEAUTY DIARY 83 EDITORIAL EDITION

STEP 1
As always, apply an eyeshadow primer to keep the shadow from creasing and make the color more vibrant.

STEP 2
Apply a lighter matte eyeshadow (try a pale pink, bone, or light yellow shade depending on your skin tone) to the inner-most corners of your eyes, the eyelid, and your brow bone. This will make your eyes appear bigger by bringing them forward.

STEP 3
Apply a darker shade of matte eyeshadow to define your crease, which will again bring your eyelids forward and make them appear larger.

STEP 4
To achieve a well-blended application, use a warmer matte shade on top of the darker shade to blend out the crease color up towards your brow bone. The gradient of color will make your eye area between your crease and brow bone appear larger.

STEP 5
Apply a warmer matte shade slightly under (not on) your lower lash line to create a soft shadow, which will make your eyes appear fuller.

STEP 6
Line your waterline with a nude or peach shade (as opposed to white) eyeliner pencil for a more natural look.

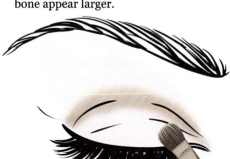

WIDER
brighter eyes

As you may know, bright colors will make something appear bigger, while dark colors will make things appear smaller. The same rings true when lining your eyes. If you are looking to give the appearance of wider, brighter eyes, follow this tip below. I personally like the look of small eyes, as it tends to look more exotic and mysterious.

STEP 7
Curl lashes and apply mascara to the top and bottom lashes.

QUICK BEAUTY TIP

FOR WIDER LOOKING EYES DON'T:

Line your eyes with a dark eyeliner.

-

Use a dark eye shadow on your eyelid.

dodge
these eyeshadow mistakes

always use eyeshadow primer
Primer helps shadow stay on longer and helps stop loose shadow from falling on your cheeks.

know your eye shape
Your eye shape will greatly determine where you should apply your shadow. Shadow placement for deep set eyes will be different than that for a hooded eye.

use a separate blending brush & blend well
Using a separate blending brush creates a more polished, gradient effect and eliminates blending too much of one color into another area of the eyes. Also, not blending enough creates defined lines between colors and screams amateur application.

pick a shadow brush based on the size of your eyes
Eyes come in many shapes and sizes, which is why it is necessary to choose an eyeshadow brush that is not too big for the size of your eyes.

use less product
Avoid applying too much product on your brush. Always give your brush a few taps to remove excess product. Start with a little and build as needed.

don't blend past your eye line
Never apply shadow past the outer portion of your eyes. When blending your shadow, stop short of the outer part of your eyes. If you happen to extend your shadow too far, do not wipe away excess shadow with a makeup sponge or tissue as this will leave a harsh line. Instead, apply a little loose powder to a clean brush to blend away. The end result should be a gradual fade.

lift your shadow
When applying your shadow, you should always try to create some type of lift (unless you're doing something extra creative).

heavy, shimmery brow bones
Some of you tend to take highlighting your brow bone to the extreme. When executing this technique, apply only a little shimmer right under the arch of your brow to act as a natural looking highlight. Don't blend the shimmer across the total brow line and do not make the highlighted area too thick.

don't use black eyeshadow to create a smoky eye
You can create a smoky eye using different shadow colors including browns, plums, dark grey, and even navy. But when using black, opt for a black eyeliner pencil for a more natural effect. Simply line with a soft eyeliner pencil (a kohl liner is ideal) across the lash line and then smudge with a firm eyeshadow brush. Make a thicker line if you want a more dramatic look.

THE BEAUTY DIARY EDITORIAL EDITION

Add a pop of color and some personality to spice up your look. Shades like bronze, a soft yellow, soft pink, and purples tend to be the more flattering colors that don't scream "Look at me, I'm trying to be creative with my makeup."

Depending on the intensity you are looking for, these looks can be created using a liquid or gel liner (for a more bold and defined look), a color eyeliner pencil (also gives definition but with softer edges), and eye shadow applied using a smudge brush (yields a softer, blended finish).

Play around with these different combinations to determine which one (if not all) you like best.

LOOK 1: UPPER LID

STEP 1
Use a metallic eyeliner pencil or eyeshadow (using a mini-shadow brush or smudge brush) and line your upper lash line. Apply it in a back and forth motion to build color to the desired intensity. Blend into the lash line. If you desire a softer line, blend out very slightly towards the crease.

STEP 2
Apply black mascara to curled upper and lower lashes.

playing with COLOR

EASY EYE LOOKS USING FUN YET PRACTICAL COLORS

LOOK 2: BOTTOM LINER

STEP 1
Use a metallic eyeliner pencil or eyeshadow (using a mini-shadow brush or smudge brush) and line your bottom lash line and waterline. Apply it in a back and forth motion to build color to the desired intensity. Blend into the lash line. If you desire a softer line, blend out very slightly towards the crease.

STEP 2
Line your upper lash line with a soft black eyeliner pencil and smudge it into your lash line.

STEP 3
Apply black mascara to curled upper and lower lashes.

LOOK 3: INNER EYE

STEP 1
Use a black eyeliner pencil, line your upper lash line, starting at the outer corner and ending half way to the center of your pupil. Then line the lower lash line, starting again at the outer corner and ending at the other side of your pupil, and smudge it into your lash line.

STEP 2
Use a metallic eyeliner pencil or eyeshadow (using a mini-shadow brush or smudge brush) and line your upper and lower lash line in the remaining eye line area. Apply it in a back and forth motion to build color to the desired intensity. Blend into the lash line and softly into the black eyeliner to eliminate any obvious ending points. If you desire a softer line, blend out very slightly towards the crease.

STEP 3
Apply black mascara to curled upper and lower lashes.

LOOK 4: OUTER EYE

STEP 1
Use black eyeliner pencil, line your upper lash line starting at the inner corner and ending halfway to the center of your pupil. Then line the lower lash line, starting again at the inner corner and ending at your pupil, and smudge it into your lash line.

STEP 2
Use a metallic eyeliner pencil or eyeshadow (using a mini-shadow brush or smudge brush) and line your upper and lower lash line in the remaining eye line area. Apply it in a back and forth motion to build color to the desired intensity. Blend into the lash line and softly into the black eyeliner to eliminate any obvious ending points. If you desire a softer line, blend out very slightly towards the crease.

STEP 3
Apply black mascara to curled upper and lower lashes.

STATEMENT EYES

This look makes a nice, bold statement with very little effort. A basic eyeshadow application paired with a bold eyeshadow color will always make a statement, but without your makeup looking like you were trying too hard to be stylish.

WHAT YOU'LL NEED:
Liquid Soft Cream Eyeshadow
Liquid Plum Eyeshadow
Black Kohl Eyeliner Pencil
Black Mascara
False Lashes (optional)

STEP 1
Line upper and lower waterline with a soft black kohl eyeliner pencil. Gently blend into lash line.

STEP 2
Apply a liquid soft cream eyeshadow onto your eyelids, your crease, and up to your brow bone.

STEP 3
In a circular motion, apply a liquid plum eyeshadow to your eyelids and up past your crease, using your fingers or eyeshadow brush.

STEP 4
Using a soft black kohl eyeliner pencil, line your eyelids and your bottom lash line. Smudge using a small eyeshadow brush.

STEP 5
Apply mascara to curled lashes. You may also apply false lashes for a more bold finish.

A NEW YORK MINUTE

I like this look because it's the perfect example of clean, fresh looking makeup. You see hints of color which bring out her natural beauty. I think this is the type of look every woman should try to achieve when wearing makeup. I'll admit, this look does take a little more than a minute, but it will get you out the door quick — you get the picture.

WHAT YOU'LL NEED:
Black Eyeliner
Soft Plum Eyeshadow
Black Mascara
Pink or Rose Lip Liner
Clear Lip Gloss
Pink Blush
Basic Eyeshadow Brush

STEP 1
With a soft black eyeliner, line only your top waterline.

STEP 2
Apply a soft plum or reddish brown shade shadow on your eyelids, fading out the crease.

STEP 3
On curled lashes, apply a light coat of mascara to the top and bottom lashes.

STEP 4
Use a soft pink or rose lip pencil to line and fill in lips. Then apply a hint of clear lip gloss.

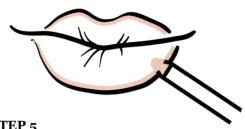

STEP 5
Then apply a hint of clear lip gloss.

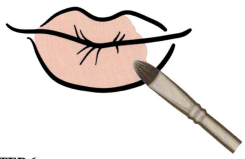

STEP 6
Apply a light dusting of pink blush to the cheeks.

SMOKIN'

For the everyday woman, a smoky eye is best kept simple. So simple, in fact, you can even wear it to work. When using this technique, it will help you avoid ending up with raccoon eyes. Also, when I am doing a smoky eye, I almost never (but not to say that you can't) do a bold lip. It tends to make the makeup look overworked and, depending on the lip color, over the top.

WHAT YOU'LL NEED:
Black Kohl Eyeliner Pencil
Nude Eyeliner Pencil (optional)
Dark Brown Shimmery Eyeshadow
Black Mascara
Peach Blush
Neutral Lip Liner (based on your skin tone)
Creamy Neutral Lipstick
Small Eyeshadow Brush

STEP 1
With a soft black eyeliner pencil, line your upper and lower waterline and work liner into your lash line. If you have small eyes you can opt for a nude eyeliner to keep your eyes from looking smaller.

STEP 2
Apply a dark brown shimmery eyeshadow on your eyelids, blending out into your crease.

STEP 3
Using a soft black kohl eyeliner pencil, line your eyelids and your bottom lash line. Smudge using a small eyeshadow brush.

STEP 4
Apply black mascara to curled upper and lower lashes.

STEP 5
Fill in lips with a creamy neutral lipstick.

STEP 6
Apply a peach blush to your cheeks

COCKTAIL GLAM

When you hear the term "evening makeup," it's usually synonymous with a dark, heavy makeup application. I think one of the biggest misconceptions is thinking you have to wear heavy makeup when it comes to an evening look.

Personally, I prefer just the opposite. This look is a perfect example of how you can wear less makeup and still make a statement. The soft gray eyeshadow adds a pop of color on the eyes and a soft, subtle lip makes it a well stated look.

WHAT YOU'LL NEED:
Nude Eyeliner
Gray Liquid Metallic Eyeshadow (or metallic eyeliner pencil)
Basic Eyeshadow Brush
Dark Brow Eyeshadow
Black Mascara
Clear Lip Gloss
Nude Lip Pencil (with a pink or rose hue)
Bronzer

STEP 1
Line your top and bottom waterline with a nude eyeliner pencil.

STEP 2
Apply gray liquid metallic eyeshadow on your lids in a circular motion, using an eyeshadow brush. Use the same color to line under your eyes. Be sure to blend well to create a gradient finish.

If you're not comfortable using liquid eyeshadow, opt for a metallic eyeliner pencil.

STEP 3
With a separate eyeshadow brush, blend a dark brown shadow into the center of the lids and blend out. Take the brush used for the gray shadow to blend away any noticeable lines.

STEP 4
Apply mascara to curled lashes, top and bottom.

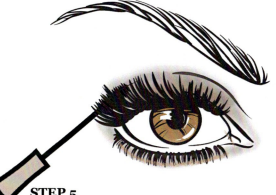

STEP 5
In this picture, the model is barley wearing any lip color. Depending on how pigmented your natural lip color is, you can go with a clear lip gloss, or opt for a nude lip pencil that contains a light rose or pink hue, followed up with clear gloss.

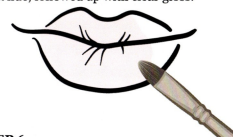

STEP 6
Finish with a warm bronzer on your cheeks.

VIBRANT THING

We all like to wear a little color sometimes, and at times even a little bit more. This look offers a vibrant pop of color using shades that are not too over the top. If you are looking for a statement eye for a day out with the girls, this is a great look to try.

WHAT YOU'LL NEED:
Black Eyeliner Pencil
Yellow Liquid Eyeshadow
Green Blue Liquid Eyeshadow
Black Mascara
Neutral Tone Lip Liner
Cream Formula Pink Lipstick
Pink Blush

STEP 1
Line your upper and lower waterline with a black eyeliner pencil, and smudge into your lash line.

STEP 2
Very lightly apply yellow liquid eyeshadow in a circular motion to your eyelids, working your way up to your crease.

STEP 3
Apply green liquid eyeshadow to your crease and the outer corners of your eyes. Then apply under your bottom lashes close to your lash line.

STEP 4
Apply black mascara to curled upper and lower lashes.

STEP 5
Line and fill in lips with a neutral tone lip liner. Apply cream formula lipstick to finish look.

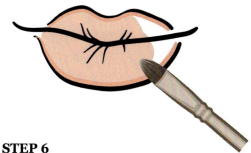

STEP 6
Blend in a pink shade blush to your cheeks.

THE BEAUTY DIARY EDITORIAL EDITION

THE MINIMALIST

It's all about enhancing your natural beauty with basic lining and defining the eyes, and adding a pop of color to the face.

WHAT YOU'LL NEED:
Tinted Moisturizer
Soft Pink Liquid Blush (or color of your choice)
Gel Eyeliner
Black Mascara
Neutral Lip Liner
Clear Lip Gloss

STEP 1
Apply a tinted moisturizer for a sheer coverage.

STEP 2
Apply a blonde or toast color eyeshadow to your eyelids.

STEP 3
Line eyes with a gel liner, creating a slight wing tip.

STEP 4
Apply black mascara to curled lashes.

STEP 5
Line lips with a neutral color lip liner.

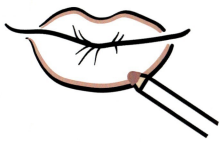

STEP 6
Apply clear lip gloss and blot away excess shine.

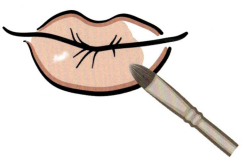

STEP 7
Dab and blend a soft pink liquid blush onto your cheeks.

THE BEAUTY DIARY 101 EDITORIAL EDITION

EBONY

This look is another modest look and works well for women with darker skin tone. As a mompreneur, I actually prefer both of these looks. My time is very limited, but I still want to present a polished look when networking and while working. This look is all about pops of pink, which makes the look fresh and pretty.

WHAT YOU'LL NEED:
Tinted Moisturizer
Black Mascara
Shimmery Pink Eyeshadow
Warm Pink Lip Liner
Soft Pink Powder Blush
Cream Formula Pink Lipstick
Shadow Brush
Lip Brush
Blush Brush

STEP 1
Apply a tinted moisturizer for a sheer coverage.

STEP 2
Apply a shimmery pink eyeshadow to your eyelids.

STEP 3
Apply black mascara to curled lashes.

STEP 4
Line lips with a warm pink lip liner.

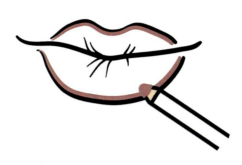

STEP 5
Apply a cream formula pink lipstick to finish the look.

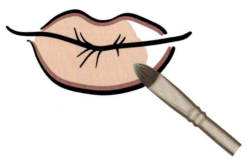

STEP 6
Brush a soft pink powder blush onto your cheeks.

THANK you

Gabriel	Thanks for giving mommy time to work on her book.
Mom & Dad	Thanks for watching Gabe while I got some work done.
San Juan	The Positive Factor!
Devon & Jordan	Thanks for reminding me how young I am.
Netro Mckay	My BFF and partner in crime. Thanks for the late night pep talks and advice.
Myss Stephens	My accountability partner. Thanks for pushing me to do better. I did it! Now it's your turn.
Lisa Zahn	For working with a sister on the editing. I hope your daughter enjoys my book.
Charlene Brown, Mindy Yang, Dr. Debra Jaliman, Alana Rivera	Thanks for your contribution and expert advice.
Tonya Broughton, Charlene Brown, Mindy Green, Wendy McAllister, Felicia Parrish	The first five to buy my book.
Glenda Freeman	For your constant words of encouragement. Love ya cuz!
All My Friends	Thanks for listening to me talk about this book. It's finally done.